50 Brazilian Pizza Recipes for Home

By: Kelly Johnson

Table of Contents

- Brazilian Margherita Pizza
- Feijoada Pizza
- Churrasco Pizza
- Bahia Shrimp Pizza
- Frango com Catupiry Pizza
- Brazilian Calabresa Pizza
- Tropical Fruit Pizza
- Queijo Coalho Pizza
- Palmito Pizza
- Muqueca Pizza
- Romeu e Julieta Pizza
- Brazilian Picanha Pizza
- São Paulo Style Pizza
- Açaí Berry Dessert Pizza
- Coxinha Inspired Pizza
- Brigadeiro Dessert Pizza
- Brazilian Pesto Pizza
- Sorvete Pizza
- Moqueca de Camarão Pizza
- Pão de Queijo Crust Pizza
- Brazilian Black Bean and Sausage Pizza
- Goiabada Pizza
- Brazilian Caprese Pizza
- Pastel de Frango Pizza
- Cachaça-Cured Salmon Pizza
- Quattro Formaggi Brazil-style
- Carioca Street Food Pizza
- Tutu à Mineira Pizza
- Brazil Nut Pesto Pizza
- Palm Heart and Bacon Pizza
- Coxinhas de Frango Pizza
- Chocotone Dessert Pizza
- Brazilian Sausage and Banana Pizza
- Mandioca Pizza
- Brazilian-Style Vegetarian Pizza

- Pork and Pineapple Pizza
- Acarajé Inspired Pizza
- Brigadeiro and Strawberry Dessert Pizza
- Brazilian Caprese Pizza
- Guava and Cream Cheese Dessert Pizza
- Brazilian-Style Clam Pizza
- Chocolate and Coconut Dessert Pizza
- Pão de Queijo Pizza Bites
- Brazilian Chicken Stroganoff Pizza
- Chocotone Bread Pudding Pizza
- Tapioca Crust Pizza
- Brazilian Chocolate and Banana Dessert Pizza
- Caipirinha Pizza
- Brazilian Nutella and Brigadeiro Dessert Pizza
- Paçoca Dessert Pizza

Brazilian Margherita Pizza

Ingredients:

- 1 pizza dough (store-bought or homemade)
- 1 cup tomato sauce
- 2 cups fresh mozzarella, sliced
- Fresh basil leaves
- Olive oil for drizzling
- Salt and pepper to taste

Instructions:

Preheat the Oven:
- Preheat your oven according to the pizza dough instructions, usually around 450°F (230°C).

Roll Out the Dough:
- Roll out the pizza dough on a floured surface to your preferred thickness.

Prepare the Pizza Pan:
- Place the rolled-out dough on a pizza pan or a baking sheet lined with parchment paper.

Add Tomato Sauce:
- Spread the tomato sauce evenly over the pizza dough, leaving a small border around the edges.

Layer Mozzarella:
- Arrange the fresh mozzarella slices evenly over the tomato sauce.

Add Fresh Basil:
- Place fresh basil leaves on top of the mozzarella, distributing them evenly.

Season and Drizzle:
- Sprinkle a pinch of salt and pepper over the pizza. Drizzle a bit of olive oil over the top for added flavor.

Bake in the Oven:
- Place the pizza in the preheated oven and bake according to the pizza dough instructions or until the crust is golden and the cheese is melted and bubbly.

Finish and Serve:
- Once the pizza is done, remove it from the oven and let it cool for a few minutes. Slice it, and serve while warm.

Optional: Customize:

- Feel free to customize the pizza with additional ingredients if desired. Some variations include adding garlic, a balsamic glaze drizzle, or a sprinkle of red pepper flakes for a bit of heat.

Enjoy your delicious Brazilian Margherita Pizza with the unique twist of fresh Brazilian flavors!

Feijoada Pizza

Ingredients:

- 1 pizza dough (store-bought or homemade)
- 1 cup black bean spread (prepared feijoada)
- 1 cup smoked sausage, sliced
- 1/2 cup bacon, cooked and crumbled
- 1 cup collard greens, chopped
- 1 cup shredded mozzarella cheese
- 2 tablespoons olive oil
- Salt and pepper to taste

Instructions:

Preheat the Oven:
- Preheat your oven according to the pizza dough instructions, usually around 450°F (230°C).

Prepare the Toppings:
- If you haven't already, cook the bacon until crispy, then crumble it. Slice the smoked sausage.

Roll Out the Dough:
- Roll out the pizza dough on a floured surface to your preferred thickness.

Prepare the Pizza Pan:
- Place the rolled-out dough on a pizza pan or a baking sheet lined with parchment paper.

Spread Black Bean Paste:
- Spread the black bean spread (feijoada) evenly over the pizza dough, leaving a small border around the edges.

Layer Sausage and Bacon:
- Distribute the sliced smoked sausage and crumbled bacon over the feijoada.

Add Collard Greens:
- Sprinkle chopped collard greens over the pizza.

Sprinkle Mozzarella:
- Evenly distribute shredded mozzarella cheese over the toppings.

Drizzle with Olive Oil:
- Drizzle olive oil over the pizza for added richness.

Season and Bake:

- Season with salt and pepper to taste. Place the pizza in the preheated oven and bake according to the pizza dough instructions or until the crust is golden and the cheese is melted.

Finish and Serve:
- Once the pizza is done, remove it from the oven, let it cool for a few minutes, then slice and serve.

Optional: Garnish:
- Garnish with additional fresh herbs, such as chopped parsley, for a burst of freshness.

Enjoy your Feijoada Pizza, a fusion of the classic Brazilian feijoada flavors on a delightful pizza crust!

Churrasco Pizza

Ingredients:

- 1 pizza dough (store-bought or homemade)
- 1 cup chimichurri sauce (recipe below)
- 1 cup grilled steak slices (prepared churrasco-style)
- 1 cup red onion, thinly sliced
- 1 cup bell peppers (assorted colors), thinly sliced
- 1 cup shredded mozzarella cheese
- Olive oil for drizzling
- Salt and pepper to taste

Chimichurri Sauce:

- 1 cup fresh parsley, finely chopped
- 1/4 cup fresh cilantro, finely chopped
- 3 cloves garlic, minced
- 1 teaspoon dried oregano
- 1/2 teaspoon red pepper flakes (adjust to taste)
- 2 tablespoons red wine vinegar
- 1/2 cup extra-virgin olive oil
- Salt and pepper to taste

Instructions:

Chimichurri Sauce:

In a bowl, combine chopped parsley, chopped cilantro, minced garlic, dried oregano, and red pepper flakes.
Add red wine vinegar and slowly whisk in the olive oil until well combined. Season with salt and pepper to taste.
Set aside the chimichurri sauce for later use.

Churrasco Pizza:

Preheat the Oven:
- Preheat your oven according to the pizza dough instructions, typically around 450°F (230°C).

Prepare the Toppings:

- Grill the steak slices to your liking, following churrasco-style preparation. Slice the grilled steak into thin strips.

Roll Out the Dough:
- Roll out the pizza dough on a floured surface to your preferred thickness.

Prepare the Pizza Pan:
- Place the rolled-out dough on a pizza pan or a baking sheet lined with parchment paper.

Spread Chimichurri Sauce:
- Spread a generous amount of chimichurri sauce over the pizza dough, leaving a small border around the edges.

Layer Steak and Vegetables:
- Distribute the grilled steak slices, thinly sliced red onion, and bell peppers over the chimichurri-covered dough.

Sprinkle Mozzarella:
- Sprinkle shredded mozzarella cheese evenly over the pizza toppings.

Drizzle with Olive Oil:
- Drizzle a bit of olive oil over the pizza for added flavor.

Season and Bake:
- Season with salt and pepper to taste. Place the pizza in the preheated oven and bake according to the pizza dough instructions or until the crust is golden and the cheese is melted.

Finish and Serve:
- Once the pizza is done, remove it from the oven, let it cool for a few minutes, then slice and serve.

Optional: Garnish with Extra Chimichurri:
- Drizzle additional chimichurri sauce over the pizza or serve extra on the side for dipping.

Enjoy your Churrasco Pizza, a delightful fusion of Brazilian barbecue flavors on a pizza!

Bahia Shrimp Pizza

Ingredients:

- 1 pizza dough (store-bought or homemade)
- 1 cup coconut milk
- 1 cup shrimp, peeled and deveined
- 1/2 cup red bell pepper, thinly sliced
- 1/2 cup green bell pepper, thinly sliced
- 1/4 cup red onion, thinly sliced
- 2 cloves garlic, minced
- 1 tablespoon dendê oil (palm oil)
- 1 tablespoon fresh cilantro, chopped
- Salt and pepper to taste
- Olive oil for drizzling
- Lime wedges for serving

Instructions:

Preheat the Oven:
- Preheat your oven according to the pizza dough instructions, usually around 450°F (230°C).

Prepare the Shrimp:
- In a pan, heat dendê oil over medium heat. Add minced garlic and sauté until fragrant.

Cook Shrimp:
- Add shrimp to the pan and cook until they turn pink, about 2-3 minutes. Season with salt and pepper. Remove from heat and set aside.

Roll Out the Dough:
- Roll out the pizza dough on a floured surface to your preferred thickness.

Prepare the Pizza Pan:
- Place the rolled-out dough on a pizza pan or a baking sheet lined with parchment paper.

Spread Coconut Milk:
- Pour coconut milk evenly over the pizza dough, leaving a small border around the edges.

Arrange Shrimp and Vegetables:
- Distribute the cooked shrimp over the coconut milk-covered dough. Scatter thinly sliced red and green bell peppers, and red onion over the pizza.

Drizzle with Olive Oil:
- Drizzle a bit of olive oil over the pizza for added richness.

Bake in the Oven:
- Place the pizza in the preheated oven and bake according to the pizza dough instructions or until the crust is golden and the toppings are cooked.

Finish and Serve:
- Once the pizza is done, remove it from the oven, sprinkle chopped cilantro on top, and let it cool for a few minutes. Slice and serve with lime wedges on the side.

Optional: Spice it Up:
- For an extra kick, you can add a touch of hot sauce or sliced chili peppers.

Enjoy your Bahia Shrimp Pizza, a taste of the vibrant and flavorful Bahian cuisine!

Frango com Catupiry Pizza

Ingredients:

- 1 pizza dough (store-bought or homemade)
- 1 cup shredded cooked chicken (seasoned with salt, pepper, and a pinch of cumin)
- 1 cup Catupiry cheese (or cream cheese as a substitute)
- 1/2 cup sweet corn kernels
- 1/4 cup green olives, sliced
- 1/4 cup fresh parsley, chopped
- Olive oil for drizzling
- Salt and pepper to taste

Instructions:

Preheat the Oven:
- Preheat your oven according to the pizza dough instructions, typically around 450°F (230°C).

Prepare the Toppings:
- Shred the cooked chicken and season it with salt, pepper, and a pinch of cumin. Slice the green olives.

Roll Out the Dough:
- Roll out the pizza dough on a floured surface to your preferred thickness.

Prepare the Pizza Pan:
- Place the rolled-out dough on a pizza pan or a baking sheet lined with parchment paper.

Spread Catupiry Cheese:
- Spread a generous layer of Catupiry cheese evenly over the pizza dough, leaving a small border around the edges.

Add Shredded Chicken:
- Distribute the seasoned shredded chicken over the Catupiry cheese.

Scatter Corn and Olives:
- Sprinkle sweet corn kernels and sliced green olives over the pizza.

Drizzle with Olive Oil:
- Drizzle a bit of olive oil over the pizza for added richness.

Season and Bake:
- Season with salt and pepper to taste. Place the pizza in the preheated oven and bake according to the pizza dough instructions or until the crust is golden and the cheese is melted.

Finish and Serve:
- Once the pizza is done, remove it from the oven, sprinkle chopped fresh parsley on top, and let it cool for a few minutes. Slice and serve.

Optional: Customize:
- Feel free to customize the pizza with additional herbs or a drizzle of hot sauce for extra flavor.

Enjoy your Frango com Catupiry Pizza—a delicious blend of shredded chicken and creamy Catupiry cheese!

Brazilian Calabresa Pizza

Ingredients:

- 1 pizza dough (store-bought or homemade)
- 1 cup tomato sauce
- 1 cup calabresa sausage, thinly sliced
- 1 cup bell peppers (assorted colors), thinly sliced
- 1/2 cup red onion, thinly sliced
- 1 cup shredded mozzarella cheese
- 2 tablespoons olive oil
- Fresh oregano leaves (or dried oregano)
- Salt and pepper to taste

Instructions:

Preheat the Oven:
- Preheat your oven according to the pizza dough instructions, typically around 450°F (230°C).

Prepare the Toppings:
- Slice the calabresa sausage thinly. Thinly slice bell peppers and red onion.

Roll Out the Dough:
- Roll out the pizza dough on a floured surface to your preferred thickness.

Prepare the Pizza Pan:
- Place the rolled-out dough on a pizza pan or a baking sheet lined with parchment paper.

Spread Tomato Sauce:
- Spread tomato sauce evenly over the pizza dough, leaving a small border around the edges.

Layer Calabresa Sausage and Vegetables:
- Distribute sliced calabresa sausage, bell peppers, and red onion evenly over the pizza.

Sprinkle Mozzarella:
- Sprinkle shredded mozzarella cheese over the toppings.

Drizzle with Olive Oil:
- Drizzle olive oil over the pizza for added flavor.

Season and Bake:
- Season with salt and pepper to taste. Place the pizza in the preheated oven and bake according to the pizza dough instructions or until the crust is golden and the cheese is melted.

Finish and Serve:

- Once the pizza is done, remove it from the oven, sprinkle fresh oregano leaves on top, and let it cool for a few minutes. Slice and serve.

Optional: Spice it Up:
- If you want an extra kick, you can add a sprinkle of red pepper flakes or a drizzle of hot sauce.

Enjoy your Brazilian Calabresa Pizza, a delightful combination of spicy sausage and vibrant vegetables!

Tropical Fruit Pizza

Ingredients:

Pizza Crust:

- 1 pre-made sugar cookie dough (store-bought or homemade)

Cream Cheese Frosting:

- 8 oz (225g) cream cheese, softened
- 1/2 cup powdered sugar
- 1 teaspoon vanilla extract

Tropical Fruit Toppings:

- 1 cup fresh pineapple, diced
- 1 cup mango, diced
- 1 cup kiwi, sliced
- 1 cup strawberries, sliced
- 1/2 cup blueberries
- 1/2 cup shredded coconut, toasted
- Mint leaves for garnish (optional)

Instructions:

Pizza Crust:

Preheat the Oven:
- Preheat your oven according to the sugar cookie dough instructions.

Roll Out the Dough:
- Roll out the sugar cookie dough on a floured surface to your preferred thickness.

Prepare the Pizza Pan:
- Place the rolled-out dough on a pizza pan or a baking sheet lined with parchment paper.

Bake the Crust:
- Follow the baking instructions for the sugar cookie dough, and bake until the crust is golden brown. Allow it to cool completely.

Cream Cheese Frosting:

Prepare the Frosting:
- In a bowl, beat together softened cream cheese, powdered sugar, and vanilla extract until smooth and creamy.

Assembling the Pizza:

Spread Cream Cheese Frosting:
- Once the cookie crust has cooled, spread the cream cheese frosting evenly over the crust, leaving a small border around the edges.

Arrange Tropical Fruits:
- Decoratively arrange diced pineapple, mango, kiwi slices, strawberry slices, and blueberries on top of the cream cheese frosting.

Sprinkle Shredded Coconut:
- Sprinkle toasted shredded coconut over the tropical fruits.

Garnish:
- Optionally, garnish with fresh mint leaves for a burst of color and flavor.

Chill and Serve:
- Chill the pizza in the refrigerator for at least 30 minutes to allow the cream cheese frosting to set. Slice and serve chilled.

Enjoy your Tropical Fruit Pizza, a delightful and visually appealing dessert that captures the vibrant flavors of tropical fruits!

Queijo Coalho Pizza

Ingredients:

- 1 pizza dough (store-bought or homemade)
- 1 cup Queijo Coalho, sliced into rounds or cubes
- 1 cup tomato sauce
- 1/4 cup fresh basil leaves, torn
- Olive oil for drizzling
- Salt and pepper to taste

Instructions:

Preheat the Oven:
- Preheat your oven according to the pizza dough instructions, usually around 450°F (230°C).

Roll Out the Dough:
- Roll out the pizza dough on a floured surface to your preferred thickness.

Prepare the Pizza Pan:
- Place the rolled-out dough on a pizza pan or a baking sheet lined with parchment paper.

Spread Tomato Sauce:
- Spread tomato sauce evenly over the pizza dough, leaving a small border around the edges.

Add Queijo Coalho:
- Place Queijo Coalho slices or cubes evenly over the tomato sauce.

Season and Drizzle:
- Season with salt and pepper to taste. Drizzle a bit of olive oil over the pizza for added richness.

Bake in the Oven:
- Place the pizza in the preheated oven and bake according to the pizza dough instructions or until the crust is golden and the Queijo Coalho is melted and slightly browned.

Finish and Garnish:
- Once the pizza is done, remove it from the oven, sprinkle torn fresh basil leaves over the top, and let it cool for a few minutes.

Slice and Serve:
- Slice the Queijo Coalho Pizza into portions and serve while warm.

Enjoy your Queijo Coalho Pizza, showcasing the distinctive taste of this Brazilian cheese! You can also add other toppings like cherry tomatoes or arugula to enhance the flavors further.

Palmito Pizza

Ingredients:

- 1 pizza dough (store-bought or homemade)
- 1 cup hearts of palm, sliced
- 1 cup tomato sauce
- 1 cup mozzarella cheese, shredded
- 1/4 cup black olives, sliced
- 1/4 cup fresh parsley, chopped
- Olive oil for drizzling
- Salt and pepper to taste

Instructions:

Preheat the Oven:
- Preheat your oven according to the pizza dough instructions, typically around 450°F (230°C).

Roll Out the Dough:
- Roll out the pizza dough on a floured surface to your preferred thickness.

Prepare the Pizza Pan:
- Place the rolled-out dough on a pizza pan or a baking sheet lined with parchment paper.

Spread Tomato Sauce:
- Spread tomato sauce evenly over the pizza dough, leaving a small border around the edges.

Add Hearts of Palm:
- Arrange sliced hearts of palm evenly over the tomato sauce.

Sprinkle Mozzarella:
- Sprinkle shredded mozzarella cheese over the hearts of palm.

Scatter Black Olives:
- Scatter sliced black olives over the pizza.

Drizzle with Olive Oil:
- Drizzle a bit of olive oil over the pizza for added flavor.

Season and Bake:
- Season with salt and pepper to taste. Place the pizza in the preheated oven and bake according to the pizza dough instructions or until the crust is golden and the cheese is melted.

Finish and Garnish:

- Once the pizza is done, remove it from the oven, sprinkle chopped fresh parsley on top, and let it cool for a few minutes.

Slice and Serve:
- Slice the Palmito Pizza into portions and serve while warm.

Enjoy your Palmito Pizza, showcasing the unique flavor of hearts of palm! You can customize it further with additional herbs or a squeeze of lemon for brightness.

Muqueca Pizza

Ingredients:

Pizza Dough:

- 1 pizza dough (store-bought or homemade)

Muqueca Sauce:

- 1 cup coconut milk
- 1 cup fish or seafood broth
- 2 tablespoons dendê oil (palm oil)
- 1 onion, finely chopped
- 2 cloves garlic, minced
- 1 red bell pepper, sliced
- 1 green bell pepper, sliced
- 1 tomato, diced
- 1 tablespoon tomato paste
- 1 teaspoon paprika
- 1 teaspoon cayenne pepper (adjust to taste)
- Salt and pepper to taste
- Fresh cilantro, chopped (for garnish)

Seafood Toppings:

- 1 cup mixed seafood (shrimp, squid, mussels, etc.)
- Olive oil for sautéing seafood

Cheese:

- 1 cup mozzarella cheese, shredded

Instructions:

Muqueca Sauce:

Prepare Muqueca Sauce:
- In a large skillet, heat dendê oil over medium heat. Add chopped onion and minced garlic, sauté until softened.

Add Vegetables:

- Add sliced red and green bell peppers, diced tomatoes, paprika, cayenne pepper, salt, and pepper. Cook until the vegetables are tender.

Create the Sauce:
- Stir in tomato paste and then pour in coconut milk and fish or seafood broth. Simmer until the sauce thickens. Adjust seasoning if needed. Set aside.

Seafood Toppings:

Cook Seafood:
- In a separate pan, heat olive oil over medium-high heat. Cook mixed seafood (shrimp, squid, mussels, etc.) until fully cooked. Set aside.

Pizza Assembly:

Preheat the Oven:
- Preheat your oven according to the pizza dough instructions, typically around 450°F (230°C).

Roll Out the Dough:
- Roll out the pizza dough on a floured surface to your preferred thickness.

Prepare the Pizza Pan:
- Place the rolled-out dough on a pizza pan or a baking sheet lined with parchment paper.

Spread Muqueca Sauce:
- Spread a generous amount of Muqueca sauce evenly over the pizza dough, leaving a small border around the edges.

Add Seafood Toppings:
- Distribute the cooked mixed seafood evenly over the Muqueca sauce.

Sprinkle Mozzarella:
- Sprinkle shredded mozzarella cheese over the seafood toppings.

Bake in the Oven:
- Place the pizza in the preheated oven and bake according to the pizza dough instructions or until the crust is golden and the cheese is melted.

Finish and Garnish:
- Once the pizza is done, remove it from the oven, sprinkle chopped fresh cilantro on top, and let it cool for a few minutes.

Slice and Serve:
- Slice the Muqueca Pizza into portions and serve while warm.

Enjoy your Muqueca Pizza, a fusion of Brazilian flavors with a creative twist!

Romeu e Julieta Pizza

Ingredients:

- 1 pizza dough (store-bought or homemade)
- 1/2 cup guava paste, thinly sliced or melted for drizzling
- 1 cup Minas cheese or cream cheese, crumbled or thinly sliced
- 2 tablespoons powdered sugar (for dusting)
- Mint leaves for garnish (optional)

Instructions:

Preheat the Oven:
- Preheat your oven according to the pizza dough instructions, typically around 450°F (230°C).

Roll Out the Dough:
- Roll out the pizza dough on a floured surface to your preferred thickness.

Prepare the Pizza Pan:
- Place the rolled-out dough on a pizza pan or a baking sheet lined with parchment paper.

Spread Guava Paste:
- If the guava paste is firm, thinly slice it. If it's soft, you can melt it slightly for drizzling. Spread the guava paste evenly over the pizza dough.

Add Cheese:
- Distribute crumbled Minas cheese or thinly sliced cream cheese over the guava paste.

Bake in the Oven:
- Place the pizza in the preheated oven and bake according to the pizza dough instructions or until the crust is golden and the cheese is slightly melted.

Finish and Garnish:
- Once the pizza is done, remove it from the oven. If you melted the guava paste, it will create a beautiful drizzle. Dust the pizza with powdered sugar.

Optional: Garnish with Mint:
- For a fresh touch, garnish the pizza with mint leaves.

Slice and Serve:
- Slice the Romeo and Juliet Pizza into portions and serve while warm.

Enjoy your Romeu e Julieta Pizza, a delightful combination of sweet guava and creamy cheese, just like the beloved Brazilian dessert!

Brazilian Picanha Pizza

Ingredients:

Pizza Dough:

- 1 pizza dough (store-bought or homemade)

Picanha Toppings:

- 1 cup picanha steak, thinly sliced
- 1 tablespoon olive oil
- 1 teaspoon smoked paprika
- 1 teaspoon garlic powder
- Salt and black pepper to taste

Other Toppings:

- 1 cup Mozzarella cheese, shredded
- 1/2 cup cherry tomatoes, halved
- 1/4 cup red onion, thinly sliced
- Fresh parsley, chopped for garnish

Chimichurri Drizzle:

- 1/4 cup fresh parsley, finely chopped
- 2 cloves garlic, minced
- 1 teaspoon dried oregano
- 1/2 teaspoon red pepper flakes
- 2 tablespoons red wine vinegar
- 1/2 cup extra-virgin olive oil
- Salt and black pepper to taste

Instructions:

Picanha Toppings:

Prepare Picanha:

- In a bowl, mix thinly sliced picanha steak with olive oil, smoked paprika, garlic powder, salt, and black pepper. Ensure the steak is well-coated.

Cook Picanha:
- In a hot skillet or grill pan, sear the picanha slices until cooked to your liking. Set aside.

Chimichurri Drizzle:

Prepare Chimichurri:
- In a bowl, combine finely chopped parsley, minced garlic, dried oregano, red pepper flakes, red wine vinegar, and extra-virgin olive oil. Season with salt and black pepper. Mix well and set aside.

Pizza Assembly:

Preheat the Oven:
- Preheat your oven according to the pizza dough instructions, typically around 450°F (230°C).

Roll Out the Dough:
- Roll out the pizza dough on a floured surface to your preferred thickness.

Prepare the Pizza Pan:
- Place the rolled-out dough on a pizza pan or a baking sheet lined with parchment paper.

Spread Mozzarella:
- Sprinkle shredded Mozzarella cheese evenly over the pizza dough.

Add Picanha and Other Toppings:
- Distribute the cooked picanha slices, halved cherry tomatoes, and thinly sliced red onion over the Mozzarella.

Bake in the Oven:
- Place the pizza in the preheated oven and bake according to the pizza dough instructions or until the crust is golden, and the cheese is melted.

Finish and Drizzle:
- Once the pizza is done, remove it from the oven. Drizzle chimichurri sauce over the top.

Garnish and Serve:
- Sprinkle chopped fresh parsley on top, slice the pizza into portions, and serve while warm.

Enjoy your Brazilian Picanha Pizza, a savory delight with the rich flavors of picanha steak and chimichurri!

São Paulo Style Pizza

Ingredients:

Pizza Dough:

- 1 pizza dough ball (store-bought or homemade)

Tomato Sauce:

- 1 cup tomato sauce
- 1 clove garlic, minced
- 1 teaspoon dried oregano
- Salt and pepper to taste

Toppings (Choose according to your preference):

- Mozzarella cheese, shredded
- Ham, thinly sliced
- Green bell peppers, thinly sliced
- Black olives, sliced
- Mushrooms, sliced
- Artichoke hearts, quartered
- Grated Parmesan cheese

Olive Oil Drizzle:

- Extra-virgin olive oil

Instructions:

Preheat the Oven:
- Preheat your oven to the highest setting, typically around 475-500°F (245-260°C).

Roll Out the Dough:
- Roll out the pizza dough on a floured surface to your preferred thickness.

Prepare the Pizza Pan:
- Place the rolled-out dough on a pizza pan or a baking sheet lined with parchment paper.

Prepare Tomato Sauce:

- In a bowl, mix tomato sauce with minced garlic, dried oregano, salt, and pepper. Spread the sauce evenly over the pizza dough, leaving a small border around the edges.

Add Toppings:
- Distribute your chosen toppings evenly over the sauce. São Paulo style pizzas often feature a combination of mozzarella, ham, bell peppers, olives, mushrooms, and artichoke hearts.

Bake in the Oven:
- Place the pizza in the preheated oven and bake until the crust is golden, and the cheese is melted and bubbly. The cooking time will vary, but it usually takes around 10-15 minutes.

Finish and Drizzle:
- Once the pizza is out of the oven, drizzle extra-virgin olive oil over the top for added flavor.

Slice and Serve:
- Allow the pizza to cool for a few minutes, then slice and serve.

Enjoy your São Paulo Style Pizza, a delightful combination of a thin crust and flavorful toppings! Feel free to customize the toppings based on your preferences.

Açaí Berry Dessert Pizza

Ingredients:

Açaí Berry Sauce:

- 1 cup frozen açaí berries (unsweetened)
- 1 banana, frozen
- 1/2 cup mixed berries (such as blueberries, strawberries)
- 2 tablespoons honey or agave nectar
- 1/4 cup coconut milk (or any milk of your choice)

Pizza Base:

- 1 pre-made sugar cookie dough (store-bought or homemade)

Toppings:

- Sliced strawberries
- Blueberries
- Shredded coconut
- Granola
- Mint leaves for garnish (optional)

Instructions:

Açaí Berry Sauce:

Prepare Açaí Berry Sauce:
- In a blender, combine frozen açaí berries, frozen banana, mixed berries, honey or agave nectar, and coconut milk. Blend until smooth and creamy. Adjust sweetness to taste.

Pizza Base:

Preheat the Oven:
- Preheat your oven according to the sugar cookie dough instructions.

Roll Out the Dough:
- Roll out the sugar cookie dough on a floured surface to your preferred thickness.

Prepare the Pizza Pan:
- Place the rolled-out dough on a pizza pan or a baking sheet lined with parchment paper.

Bake the Crust:
- Follow the baking instructions for the sugar cookie dough, and bake until the crust is golden brown. Allow it to cool completely.

Pizza Assembly:

Spread Açaí Berry Sauce:
- Once the cookie crust has cooled, spread the Açaí Berry sauce evenly over the crust, leaving a small border around the edges.

Add Fresh Toppings:
- Decorate the pizza with sliced strawberries, blueberries, shredded coconut, and granola. Get creative with the arrangement.

Garnish:
- Optionally, garnish the pizza with fresh mint leaves for a burst of color and flavor.

Slice and Serve:
- Slice the Açaí Berry Dessert Pizza into portions and serve immediately.

Enjoy your Açaí Berry Dessert Pizza, a healthy and delicious treat with the vibrant flavors of açaí berries and an assortment of delightful toppings!

Coxinha Inspired Pizza

Ingredients:

Pizza Dough:

- 1 pizza dough ball (store-bought or homemade)

Creamy Chicken Filling:

- 1 cup shredded cooked chicken
- 1/2 cup cream cheese
- 1/4 cup mayonnaise
- 1 clove garlic, minced
- 1 tablespoon chopped fresh parsley
- Salt and pepper to taste

Toppings:

- 1 cup Mozzarella cheese, shredded
- 1/2 cup catupiry cheese (or cream cheese as a substitute)
- 1/4 cup green onions, chopped
- 1/4 cup black olives, sliced
- 1/4 cup corn kernels
- 1/4 cup cherry tomatoes, halved

Coxinha Dough Crust:

- 1/2 cup flour (for dusting)
- 1 cup coxinha dough (you can use a coxinha recipe to make the dough)

Instructions:

Preheat the Oven:
- Preheat your oven to the highest setting, typically around 475-500°F (245-260°C).

Roll Out the Pizza Dough:
- Roll out the pizza dough on a floured surface to your preferred thickness.

Prepare Creamy Chicken Filling:

- In a bowl, mix shredded cooked chicken, cream cheese, mayonnaise, minced garlic, chopped fresh parsley, salt, and pepper. This will be the pizza sauce.

Prepare Coxinha Dough Crust:
- Roll out coxinha dough on a floured surface to create a thin layer. This will act as a crust. Dust with flour as needed to prevent sticking.

Assemble the Pizza:
- Place the rolled-out pizza dough on a pizza pan or a baking sheet lined with parchment paper. Lay the coxinha dough crust over the pizza dough.

Spread Creamy Chicken Filling:
- Spread the creamy chicken filling evenly over the coxinha dough crust.

Add Toppings:
- Sprinkle Mozzarella cheese over the chicken filling. Add dollops of catupiry cheese (or cream cheese), chopped green onions, sliced black olives, corn kernels, and halved cherry tomatoes.

Bake in the Oven:
- Place the pizza in the preheated oven and bake until the crust is golden, and the cheese is melted and bubbly. The cooking time will vary but usually takes around 12-15 minutes.

Finish and Serve:
- Once the pizza is out of the oven, let it cool for a few minutes. Slice and serve.

Enjoy your Coxinha-Inspired Pizza, a creative fusion of Brazilian coxinha flavors with the comfort of a pizza!

Brigadeiro Dessert Pizza

Ingredients:

Pizza Dough:

- 1 pizza dough ball (store-bought or homemade)

Brigadeiro Sauce:

- 1 can (14 ounces) sweetened condensed milk
- 2 tablespoons unsweetened cocoa powder
- 2 tablespoons unsalted butter
- Chocolate sprinkles for topping

Toppings:

- 1/2 cup shredded coconut, toasted
- Sliced strawberries
- Sliced bananas
- Chopped nuts (e.g., pistachios or hazelnuts)

Additional:

- Sweetened condensed milk (for drizzling)

Instructions:

Preheat the Oven:
- Preheat your oven to the temperature recommended for the pizza dough, usually around 450°F (230°C).

Roll Out the Pizza Dough:
- Roll out the pizza dough on a floured surface to your preferred thickness.

Prepare Brigadeiro Sauce:
- In a saucepan over medium heat, combine sweetened condensed milk, cocoa powder, and butter. Stir continuously until the mixture thickens and pulls away from the sides of the pan to form a soft, fudgy consistency. Remove from heat and let it cool slightly.

Assemble the Pizza:

- Place the rolled-out pizza dough on a pizza pan or a baking sheet lined with parchment paper.

Spread Brigadeiro Sauce:
- Spread the brigadeiro sauce evenly over the pizza dough, leaving a small border around the edges.

Add Toppings:
- Sprinkle toasted shredded coconut over the brigadeiro sauce. Add sliced strawberries, sliced bananas, and chopped nuts.

Bake in the Oven:
- Place the pizza in the preheated oven and bake according to the pizza dough instructions or until the crust is golden.

Finish and Drizzle:
- Once the pizza is out of the oven, drizzle additional sweetened condensed milk over the top for extra sweetness.

Slice and Serve:
- Let the Brigadeiro Dessert Pizza cool for a few minutes, then slice and serve.

Enjoy your Brigadeiro Dessert Pizza, a delightful combination of chocolatey brigadeiro goodness with the fun twist of a pizza!

Brazilian Pesto Pizza

Ingredients:

Pizza Dough:

- 1 pizza dough ball (store-bought or homemade)

Brazilian Pesto Sauce:

- 2 cups fresh basil leaves
- 1/2 cup cilantro leaves
- 1/2 cup Brazilian nuts (or substitute with cashews or pine nuts)
- 2 cloves garlic, peeled
- 1/2 cup Parmesan cheese, grated
- 1/2 cup Pecorino cheese, grated
- 1 cup extra-virgin olive oil
- Salt and black pepper to taste
- Juice of 1 lime

Toppings:

- 1 cup Mozzarella cheese, shredded
- Cherry tomatoes, halved
- 1/4 cup black olives, sliced
- 1/4 cup red onion, thinly sliced
- Arugula leaves for topping

Additional:

- Olive oil for drizzling

Instructions:

Preheat the Oven:
- Preheat your oven to the temperature recommended for the pizza dough, usually around 450°F (230°C).

Roll Out the Pizza Dough:
- Roll out the pizza dough on a floured surface to your preferred thickness.

Prepare Brazilian Pesto Sauce:

- In a food processor, combine fresh basil, cilantro, Brazilian nuts, garlic, Parmesan cheese, Pecorino cheese, and lime juice. Pulse until ingredients are finely chopped.
- While the food processor is running, gradually drizzle in the olive oil until the pesto reaches a smooth consistency. Season with salt and black pepper to taste. Set aside.

Assemble the Pizza:
- Place the rolled-out pizza dough on a pizza pan or a baking sheet lined with parchment paper.

Spread Brazilian Pesto Sauce:
- Spread a generous amount of Brazilian pesto sauce evenly over the pizza dough, leaving a small border around the edges.

Add Toppings:
- Sprinkle shredded Mozzarella cheese over the pesto. Add halved cherry tomatoes, sliced black olives, and thinly sliced red onion.

Bake in the Oven:
- Place the pizza in the preheated oven and bake according to the pizza dough instructions or until the crust is golden, and the cheese is melted.

Finish and Garnish:
- Once the pizza is out of the oven, drizzle a bit of olive oil over the top. Top with fresh arugula leaves for a peppery finish.

Slice and Serve:
- Let the Brazilian Pesto Pizza cool for a few minutes, then slice and serve.

Enjoy your Brazilian Pesto Pizza, a delightful combination of fresh herbs, nuts, and cheese, inspired by the vibrant flavors of Brazil!

Sorvete Pizza

Ingredients:

Pizza Cookie Crust:

- 1 package of pre-made chocolate chip cookie dough (or your favorite cookie dough)

Ice Cream and Toppings:

- 2 pints of your favorite ice cream flavors
- Chocolate sauce
- Caramel sauce
- Whipped cream
- Assorted toppings (sprinkles, nuts, chocolate chips, fruit, etc.)

Instructions:

Preheat the Oven:
- Preheat your oven according to the instructions on the cookie dough package.

Prepare the Cookie Crust:
- Press the cookie dough evenly onto a pizza pan or a baking sheet lined with parchment paper, creating a large cookie crust. Follow the package instructions for baking or until the crust is golden brown.

Cool the Cookie Crust:
- Allow the cookie crust to cool completely. You can place it in the refrigerator to speed up the cooling process.

Prepare the Ice Cream:
- Soften the ice cream by letting it sit at room temperature for a few minutes. You can also briefly microwave it, but be careful not to melt it completely.

Spread Ice Cream:
- Once the cookie crust is cooled, spread a layer of softened ice cream over the cookie, covering it evenly. You can use one flavor or create a combination of your favorite flavors.

Add Toppings:
- Drizzle chocolate sauce and caramel sauce over the ice cream. Sprinkle your favorite toppings such as nuts, chocolate chips, and sprinkles.

Freeze:
- Place the Sorvete Pizza in the freezer for at least 2-3 hours, or until the ice cream is firm.

Serve:
- Before serving, let the Sorvete Pizza sit at room temperature for a few minutes to make it easier to slice. Garnish with whipped cream.

Slice and Enjoy:
- Slice the Sorvete Pizza into wedges, just like a regular pizza, and enjoy this delightful and refreshing dessert.

Feel free to get creative with your choice of ice cream flavors and toppings to make it uniquely yours!

Moqueca de Camarão Pizza

Ingredients:

Pizza Dough:

- 1 pizza dough (store-bought or homemade)

Moqueca de Camarão Sauce:

- 1 pound (about 500g) shrimp, peeled and deveined
- 1 cup coconut milk
- 1 cup fish or shrimp broth
- 1 onion, finely chopped
- 3 cloves garlic, minced
- 1 red bell pepper, sliced
- 1 green bell pepper, sliced
- 1 tomato, diced
- 2 tablespoons tomato paste
- 1 tablespoon palm oil (dendê oil)
- 1 tablespoon olive oil
- 1 teaspoon sweet paprika
- 1 teaspoon cayenne pepper (adjust to taste)
- Salt and pepper to taste
- Fresh cilantro, chopped (for garnish)

Toppings:

- Mozzarella cheese, shredded
- Sliced red onion
- Sliced bell peppers (assorted colors)
- Cherry tomatoes, halved

Instructions:

Moqueca de Camarão Sauce:

Prepare Moqueca Sauce:
- In a large skillet, heat olive oil and palm oil over medium heat. Add chopped onion and minced garlic, sauté until softened.

Add Vegetables:
- Add sliced red and green bell peppers, diced tomatoes, sweet paprika, cayenne pepper, salt, and pepper. Cook until the vegetables are tender.

Create the Sauce:
- Stir in tomato paste, coconut milk, and fish or shrimp broth. Simmer until the sauce thickens. Adjust seasoning if needed.

Add Shrimp:
- Add the peeled and deveined shrimp to the sauce. Cook until the shrimp are opaque and cooked through. Remove from heat, and set aside.

Pizza Assembly:

Preheat the Oven:
- Preheat your oven according to the pizza dough instructions, typically around 450°F (230°C).

Roll Out the Dough:
- Roll out the pizza dough on a floured surface to your preferred thickness.

Prepare the Pizza Pan:
- Place the rolled-out dough on a pizza pan or a baking sheet lined with parchment paper.

Spread Moqueca Sauce:
- Spread a generous amount of Moqueca de Camarão sauce evenly over the pizza dough, leaving a small border around the edges.

Add Toppings:
- Sprinkle shredded Mozzarella cheese over the sauce. Add sliced red onion, sliced bell peppers, and halved cherry tomatoes.

Bake in the Oven:
- Place the pizza in the preheated oven and bake according to the pizza dough instructions or until the crust is golden and the cheese is melted.

Finish and Garnish:
- Once the pizza is done, remove it from the oven, sprinkle chopped fresh cilantro on top, and let it cool for a few minutes.

Slice and Serve:
- Slice the Moqueca de Camarão Pizza into portions and serve while warm.

Enjoy your Moqueca de Camarão Pizza, a delightful fusion of Brazilian seafood stew flavors with the comforting appeal of pizza!

Pão de Queijo Crust Pizza

Ingredients:

Pão de Queijo Crust:

- 2 cups tapioca flour (polvilho azedo)
- 1 cup milk
- 1/2 cup unsalted butter
- 1 teaspoon salt
- 1 1/2 cups grated Parmesan cheese
- 1 1/2 cups grated Mozzarella cheese
- 2 large eggs

Pizza Toppings:

- Tomato sauce
- Mozzarella cheese, shredded
- Sliced pepperoni
- Sliced bell peppers
- Sliced black olives
- Fresh basil leaves

Instructions:

Pão de Queijo Crust:

Preheat the Oven:
- Preheat your oven to 375°F (190°C).

Prepare Pão de Queijo Dough:
- In a saucepan, combine milk, butter, and salt. Heat over medium heat until the mixture comes to a gentle boil.

Mix Tapioca Flour:
- In a large mixing bowl, place tapioca flour. Pour the hot milk mixture over the tapioca flour and stir until well combined.

Add Cheese and Eggs:
- Allow the mixture to cool slightly. Add grated Parmesan and Mozzarella cheese, mixing well. Then, add the eggs one at a time, incorporating each one thoroughly.

Form Dough:

- The mixture will form a sticky dough. Allow it to rest for about 15 minutes until it's cool enough to handle.

Shape the Pão de Queijo Crust:
- Divide the dough into two portions. On a surface dusted with tapioca flour, shape each portion into a ball and flatten it into a round pizza crust shape. Use tapioca flour to prevent sticking.

Bake the Crust:
- Place the shaped crusts on a baking sheet lined with parchment paper. Bake in the preheated oven for about 15-20 minutes or until the edges are golden.

Pizza Assembly:

Preheat the Oven:
- Adjust your oven temperature to 425°F (220°C).

Add Pizza Toppings:
- Remove the partially baked Pão de Queijo crusts from the oven. Spread tomato sauce over the crusts and add shredded Mozzarella cheese, pepperoni slices, sliced bell peppers, black olives, and any other desired toppings.

Bake the Pizza:
- Return the topped pizzas to the oven and bake for an additional 10-15 minutes, or until the cheese is melted and bubbly, and the edges are golden.

Finish and Serve:
- Once done, remove from the oven, garnish with fresh basil leaves, slice, and serve immediately.

Enjoy your Pão de Queijo Crust Pizza, a delicious blend of the Brazilian cheese bread flavor with the classic pizza experience!

Brazilian Black Bean and Sausage Pizza

Ingredients:

Pizza Dough:

- 1 pizza dough (store-bought or homemade)

Black Bean Spread:

- 1 can (15 ounces) black beans, drained and rinsed
- 2 tablespoons olive oil
- 2 cloves garlic, minced
- 1 teaspoon ground cumin
- Salt and pepper to taste
- 1 tablespoon fresh lime juice

Toppings:

- 1 cup cooked and sliced Brazilian sausage (linguiça) or chorizo
- 1 cup Mozzarella cheese, shredded
- 1/2 cup red onion, thinly sliced
- 1/4 cup fresh cilantro, chopped
- 1/4 cup black olives, sliced
- Jalapeño slices (optional, for heat)

Avocado Cream Drizzle:

- 1 ripe avocado, peeled and pitted
- 1/4 cup sour cream
- 1 tablespoon fresh lime juice
- Salt and pepper to taste

Instructions:

Black Bean Spread:

Prepare Black Bean Spread:

- In a food processor, combine black beans, olive oil, minced garlic, ground cumin, salt, pepper, and fresh lime juice. Blend until smooth. Adjust seasoning to taste.

Avocado Cream Drizzle:

Prepare Avocado Cream:
- In a separate bowl, mash the ripe avocado. Stir in sour cream, fresh lime juice, salt, and pepper until well combined. Set aside.

Pizza Assembly:

Preheat the Oven:
- Preheat your oven according to the pizza dough instructions, typically around 450°F (230°C).

Roll Out the Dough:
- Roll out the pizza dough on a floured surface to your preferred thickness.

Prepare the Pizza Pan:
- Place the rolled-out dough on a pizza pan or a baking sheet lined with parchment paper.

Spread Black Bean Spread:
- Spread the black bean mixture evenly over the pizza dough, leaving a small border around the edges.

Add Toppings:
- Distribute cooked and sliced Brazilian sausage or chorizo over the black bean spread. Sprinkle shredded Mozzarella cheese, thinly sliced red onion, chopped fresh cilantro, black olive slices, and jalapeño slices (if using).

Bake in the Oven:
- Place the pizza in the preheated oven and bake according to the pizza dough instructions or until the crust is golden, and the cheese is melted.

Finish and Drizzle:
- Once the pizza is done, remove it from the oven. Drizzle the prepared avocado cream over the top.

Slice and Serve:
- Slice the Brazilian Black Bean and Sausage Pizza into portions and serve while warm.

Enjoy your unique and delicious Brazilian-inspired pizza!

Goiabada Pizza

Ingredients:

Pizza Dough:

- 1 pizza dough (store-bought or homemade)

Goiabada Topping:

- 1 cup goiabada (Brazilian guava paste), sliced or grated
- 1/4 cup cream cheese, softened
- 1 tablespoon honey or agave syrup (optional, for drizzling)

Other Toppings (Optional):

- Shredded coconut
- Sliced bananas
- Chopped nuts (e.g., walnuts or pistachios)

Instructions:

Preheat the Oven:
- Preheat your oven according to the pizza dough instructions, typically around 450°F (230°C).

Roll Out the Dough:
- Roll out the pizza dough on a floured surface to your preferred thickness.

Prepare the Pizza Pan:
- Place the rolled-out dough on a pizza pan or a baking sheet lined with parchment paper.

Spread Cream Cheese:
- Spread softened cream cheese evenly over the pizza dough, leaving a small border around the edges.

Arrange Goiabada:
- Distribute sliced or grated goiabada over the cream cheese layer. Ensure an even distribution to cover the pizza.

Add Additional Toppings (Optional):
- If desired, sprinkle shredded coconut, sliced bananas, or chopped nuts over the goiabada layer.

Bake in the Oven:

- Place the pizza in the preheated oven and bake according to the pizza dough instructions or until the crust is golden.

Drizzle with Honey (Optional):
- If you'd like to add a touch of sweetness, drizzle honey or agave syrup over the top of the finished pizza.

Slice and Serve:
- Once the Goiabada Pizza is done, remove it from the oven. Allow it to cool for a few minutes, then slice and serve.

Enjoy your Goiabada Pizza, a delicious fusion of the sweet and tropical flavors of guava paste on a pizza crust!

Brazilian Caprese Pizza

Ingredients:

Pizza Dough:

- 1 pizza dough (store-bought or homemade)

Toppings:

- 1 cup cherry tomatoes, halved
- 1 cup fresh Mozzarella cheese, sliced or torn into pieces
- 1/4 cup black olives, sliced
- 1/4 cup fresh basil leaves, torn
- 1/4 cup Brazilian pesto (recipe below)
- Balsamic glaze (for drizzling)
- Salt and black pepper to taste

Brazilian Pesto:

- 2 cups fresh basil leaves
- 1/2 cup Brazilian nuts (or substitute with cashews or pine nuts)
- 2 cloves garlic, minced
- 1/2 cup Parmesan cheese, grated
- 1/2 cup Pecorino cheese, grated
- 1 cup extra-virgin olive oil
- Salt and black pepper to taste
- Juice of 1 lime

Instructions:

Brazilian Pesto:

Prepare Brazilian Pesto:
- In a food processor, combine fresh basil, Brazilian nuts, minced garlic, Parmesan cheese, Pecorino cheese, and lime juice. Pulse until ingredients are finely chopped.

Create the Pesto:
- While the food processor is running, gradually drizzle in the olive oil until the pesto reaches a smooth consistency. Season with salt and black pepper to taste. Set aside.

Pizza Assembly:

Preheat the Oven:
- Preheat your oven according to the pizza dough instructions, typically around 450°F (230°C).

Roll Out the Dough:
- Roll out the pizza dough on a floured surface to your preferred thickness.

Prepare the Pizza Pan:
- Place the rolled-out dough on a pizza pan or a baking sheet lined with parchment paper.

Spread Brazilian Pesto:
- Spread a generous amount of Brazilian pesto evenly over the pizza dough, leaving a small border around the edges.

Add Caprese Toppings:
- Arrange halved cherry tomatoes and fresh Mozzarella cheese over the pesto. Sprinkle sliced black olives and torn fresh basil leaves on top. Season with salt and black pepper.

Bake in the Oven:
- Place the pizza in the preheated oven and bake according to the pizza dough instructions or until the crust is golden, and the cheese is melted.

Drizzle with Balsamic Glaze:
- Once the pizza is done, remove it from the oven. Drizzle with balsamic glaze for an extra burst of flavor.

Slice and Serve:
- Slice the Brazilian Caprese Pizza into portions and serve while warm.

Enjoy your Brazilian Caprese Pizza, a delicious blend of fresh and vibrant flavors!

Pastel de Frango Pizza

Ingredients:

Pizza Dough:

- 1 pizza dough (store-bought or homemade)

Chicken Filling:

- 1 cup shredded cooked chicken
- 1/2 cup cream cheese
- 1/4 cup mayonnaise
- 1 clove garlic, minced
- 1 tablespoon chopped fresh cilantro
- Salt and pepper to taste

Toppings:

- 1 cup Mozzarella cheese, shredded
- Sliced red bell pepper
- Sliced green bell pepper
- Sliced red onion
- Sliced black olives

Catupiry Drizzle:

- 1/2 cup Catupiry cheese (or substitute with cream cheese)
- 2 tablespoons heavy cream

Instructions:

Chicken Filling:

Prepare Chicken Filling:
- In a bowl, mix shredded cooked chicken, cream cheese, mayonnaise, minced garlic, chopped fresh cilantro, salt, and pepper. Set aside.

Catupiry Drizzle:

Prepare Catupiry Drizzle:
- In a small saucepan, heat Catupiry cheese (or cream cheese) with heavy cream over low heat. Stir until well combined and smooth. Set aside.

Pizza Assembly:

Preheat the Oven:
- Preheat your oven according to the pizza dough instructions, typically around 450°F (230°C).

Roll Out the Dough:
- Roll out the pizza dough on a floured surface to your preferred thickness.

Prepare the Pizza Pan:
- Place the rolled-out dough on a pizza pan or a baking sheet lined with parchment paper.

Spread Chicken Filling:
- Spread the chicken filling evenly over the pizza dough, leaving a small border around the edges.

Add Toppings:
- Sprinkle shredded Mozzarella cheese over the chicken filling. Add sliced red and green bell peppers, sliced red onion, and black olives.

Bake in the Oven:
- Place the pizza in the preheated oven and bake according to the pizza dough instructions or until the crust is golden, and the cheese is melted.

Drizzle with Catupiry:
- Once the pizza is done, remove it from the oven. Drizzle the prepared Catupiry mixture over the top.

Slice and Serve:
- Slice the Pastel de Frango Pizza into portions and serve while warm.

Enjoy your delicious Pastel de Frango Pizza, a creative fusion of Brazilian pastel and pizza flavors!

Cachaça-Cured Salmon Pizza

Ingredients:

Pizza Dough:

- 1 pizza dough (store-bought or homemade)

Cachaça-Cured Salmon:

- 8 oz (about 225g) fresh salmon fillet, skinless and boneless
- 2 tablespoons cachaça
- 1 tablespoon coarse salt (kosher or sea salt)
- 1 tablespoon granulated sugar
- Zest of 1 lime
- Freshly ground black pepper to taste

Toppings:

- 1/2 cup crème fraîche or sour cream
- 1 tablespoon Dijon mustard
- 1 tablespoon fresh dill, chopped
- Red onion, thinly sliced
- Capers
- Arugula leaves
- Lemon wedges (for serving)

Instructions:

Cachaça-Cured Salmon:

Prepare Cachaça-Cured Salmon:
- In a small bowl, mix cachaça, coarse salt, sugar, lime zest, and black pepper to create the curing mixture.

Cure Salmon:
- Place the salmon fillet on a piece of plastic wrap. Spread the curing mixture evenly over the salmon, ensuring it's well-coated. Wrap the salmon tightly in plastic wrap.

Refrigerate:

- Place the wrapped salmon in the refrigerator and let it cure for at least 24 hours. Flip the salmon halfway through the curing process.

Slice Salmon Thin:
- After curing, unwrap the salmon and thinly slice it. The slices are now ready to be used as a topping for the pizza.

Pizza Assembly:

Preheat the Oven:
- Preheat your oven according to the pizza dough instructions, typically around 450°F (230°C).

Roll Out the Dough:
- Roll out the pizza dough on a floured surface to your preferred thickness.

Prepare the Pizza Pan:
- Place the rolled-out dough on a pizza pan or a baking sheet lined with parchment paper.

Mix Crème Fraîche Mixture:
- In a small bowl, mix crème fraîche or sour cream with Dijon mustard and chopped fresh dill.

Assemble the Pizza:
- Spread the crème fraîche mixture evenly over the pizza dough. Arrange the thinly sliced cachaça-cured salmon on top.

Add Toppings:
- Scatter red onion slices, capers, and arugula leaves over the cured salmon.

Bake in the Oven:
- Place the pizza in the preheated oven and bake according to the pizza dough instructions or until the crust is golden.

Finish and Serve:
- Once the pizza is done, remove it from the oven. Squeeze fresh lemon juice over the top, slice, and serve.

Enjoy your Cachaça-Cured Salmon Pizza, a sophisticated and flavorful dish with Brazilian-inspired elements!

Quattro Formaggi Brazil-style

Ingredients:

Pizza Dough:

- 1 pizza dough (store-bought or homemade)

Cheese Blend:

- 1/2 cup Minas cheese, grated (or substitute with a mild white cheese like mozzarella)
- 1/2 cup Queijo Prato (Brazilian cheese similar to Edam), shredded
- 1/2 cup Catupiry cheese (or cream cheese)
- 1/2 cup Parmesan cheese, grated

Toppings:

- 1/4 cup cherry tomatoes, halved
- Fresh oregano leaves
- Brazilian honey (optional, for drizzling)

Instructions:

Preheat the Oven:
- Preheat your oven according to the pizza dough instructions, typically around 450°F (230°C).

Roll Out the Dough:
- Roll out the pizza dough on a floured surface to your preferred thickness.

Prepare the Pizza Pan:
- Place the rolled-out dough on a pizza pan or a baking sheet lined with parchment paper.

Create the Cheese Blend:
- In a bowl, mix together the grated Minas cheese, shredded Queijo Prato, Catupiry cheese (or cream cheese), and grated Parmesan cheese. This blend will serve as the four cheeses for your pizza.

Spread Cheese Blend:
- Evenly spread the four-cheese blend over the pizza dough, ensuring full coverage.

Add Toppings:

- Scatter halved cherry tomatoes over the cheese blend. Sprinkle fresh oregano leaves on top.

Bake in the Oven:
- Place the pizza in the preheated oven and bake according to the pizza dough instructions or until the crust is golden, and the cheese is melted and bubbly.

Drizzle with Brazilian Honey (Optional):
- For an extra touch of sweetness, you can drizzle a bit of Brazilian honey over the top after the pizza comes out of the oven.

Slice and Serve:
- Once the Quattro Formaggi Brazil-style Pizza is done, remove it from the oven, slice, and serve immediately.

Enjoy your Quattro Formaggi Brazil-style Pizza, a cheesy delight with a Brazilian twist!

Carioca Street Food Pizza

Ingredients:

Pizza Dough:

- 1 pizza dough (store-bought or homemade)

Carioca Toppings:

- 1 cup shredded cooked chicken
- 1/2 cup Brazilian cream cheese (requeijão)
- 1/2 cup shredded Minas cheese (or mozzarella)
- 1/4 cup corn kernels
- 1/4 cup diced tomatoes
- 1/4 cup chopped green onions
- 1/4 cup chopped fresh cilantro
- 1/4 cup black beans, cooked and drained
- 1/4 cup sliced black olives
- Salt and black pepper to taste

Cilantro-Lime Drizzle:

- 1/4 cup fresh cilantro, chopped
- Zest and juice of 1 lime
- 2 tablespoons olive oil
- Salt and pepper to taste

Instructions:

Cilantro-Lime Drizzle:

Prepare Cilantro-Lime Drizzle:
- In a small bowl, combine chopped cilantro, lime zest, lime juice, olive oil, salt, and pepper. Set aside for drizzling over the finished pizza.

Pizza Assembly:

Preheat the Oven:

- Preheat your oven according to the pizza dough instructions, typically around 450°F (230°C).

Roll Out the Dough:
- Roll out the pizza dough on a floured surface to your preferred thickness.

Prepare the Pizza Pan:
- Place the rolled-out dough on a pizza pan or a baking sheet lined with parchment paper.

Spread Carioca Toppings:
- Evenly spread Brazilian cream cheese (requeijão) over the pizza dough, leaving a small border around the edges.

Add Chicken and Vegetables:
- Distribute shredded cooked chicken over the cream cheese. Sprinkle shredded Minas cheese (or mozzarella) on top. Add corn kernels, diced tomatoes, chopped green onions, chopped fresh cilantro, black beans, and sliced black olives. Season with salt and black pepper.

Bake in the Oven:
- Place the pizza in the preheated oven and bake according to the pizza dough instructions or until the crust is golden, and the cheese is melted.

Drizzle with Cilantro-Lime Sauce:
- Once the pizza is done, remove it from the oven. Drizzle the prepared cilantro-lime sauce over the top.

Slice and Serve:
- Slice the Carioca Street Food Pizza into portions and serve while warm.

Enjoy your Carioca Street Food Pizza, a burst of flavors inspired by the lively street food scene in Rio de Janeiro!

Tutu à Mineira Pizza

Ingredients:

Pizza Dough:

- 1 pizza dough (store-bought or homemade)

Tutu à Mineira Sauce:

- 1 cup cooked black beans, drained
- 1 cup cassava flour (farinha de mandioca)
- 1/2 cup bacon, diced
- 1/2 cup sausage, sliced
- 1/2 cup collard greens, finely chopped
- 1/2 cup onions, finely chopped
- 3 cloves garlic, minced
- 2 tablespoons vegetable oil
- Salt and pepper to taste

Toppings:

- 1 cup Queijo Minas cheese (or substitute with mozzarella), shredded
- 1/4 cup fresh parsley, chopped
- Olive oil for drizzling

Instructions:

Tutu à Mineira Sauce:

Prepare Tutu à Mineira Sauce:
- In a large skillet, heat vegetable oil over medium heat. Add diced bacon and sliced sausage. Cook until the bacon is crispy and the sausage is browned.

Add Vegetables:
- Add finely chopped collard greens, onions, and minced garlic to the skillet. Sauté until the vegetables are tender.

Mix in Black Beans:
- Stir in the cooked black beans, mixing well with the vegetable and meat mixture.

Add Cassava Flour:
- Gradually add cassava flour (farinha de mandioca) to the skillet, stirring continuously to combine. Cook until the mixture thickens to a consistency similar to a thick porridge. Season with salt and pepper to taste. Set aside.

Pizza Assembly:

Preheat the Oven:
- Preheat your oven according to the pizza dough instructions, typically around 450°F (230°C).

Roll Out the Dough:
- Roll out the pizza dough on a floured surface to your preferred thickness.

Prepare the Pizza Pan:
- Place the rolled-out dough on a pizza pan or a baking sheet lined with parchment paper.

Spread Tutu à Mineira Sauce:
- Spread the Tutu à Mineira sauce evenly over the pizza dough, leaving a small border around the edges.

Add Cheese and Toppings:
- Sprinkle shredded Queijo Minas cheese (or mozzarella) over the Tutu à Mineira sauce. Add fresh parsley on top.

Bake in the Oven:
- Place the pizza in the preheated oven and bake according to the pizza dough instructions or until the crust is golden, and the cheese is melted and bubbly.

Drizzle with Olive Oil:
- Once the pizza is done, remove it from the oven. Drizzle with a bit of olive oil for added flavor.

Slice and Serve:
- Slice the Tutu à Mineira Pizza into portions and serve while warm.

Enjoy your Tutu à Mineira Pizza, a delightful fusion of Brazilian flavors with the creativity of pizza!

Brazil Nut Pesto Pizza

Ingredients:

Pizza Dough:

- 1 pizza dough (store-bought or homemade)

Brazil Nut Pesto:

- 1 cup Brazil nuts, toasted
- 2 cups fresh basil leaves
- 3 cloves garlic
- 1/2 cup Parmesan cheese, grated
- 1/2 cup Pecorino cheese, grated
- 1 cup extra-virgin olive oil
- Salt and black pepper to taste
- Juice of 1 lemon

Toppings:

- 1 cup cherry tomatoes, halved
- 1 cup Mozzarella cheese, shredded
- 1/4 cup Kalamata olives, sliced
- 1/4 cup red onion, thinly sliced
- Fresh arugula for topping (optional)
- Red pepper flakes (optional, for heat)

Instructions:

Brazil Nut Pesto:

Toast Brazil Nuts:
- In a dry skillet, toast Brazil nuts over medium heat until fragrant. Allow them to cool.

Prepare Brazil Nut Pesto:
- In a food processor, combine toasted Brazil nuts, fresh basil leaves, garlic, Parmesan cheese, Pecorino cheese, and lemon juice. Pulse until the mixture is coarsely ground.

Drizzle Olive Oil:

- With the food processor running, gradually drizzle in the olive oil until the pesto reaches a smooth consistency. Season with salt and black pepper to taste. Set aside.

Pizza Assembly:

Preheat the Oven:
- Preheat your oven according to the pizza dough instructions, typically around 450°F (230°C).

Roll Out the Dough:
- Roll out the pizza dough on a floured surface to your preferred thickness.

Prepare the Pizza Pan:
- Place the rolled-out dough on a pizza pan or a baking sheet lined with parchment paper.

Spread Brazil Nut Pesto:
- Evenly spread a generous amount of Brazil Nut Pesto over the pizza dough, leaving a small border around the edges.

Add Toppings:
- Distribute halved cherry tomatoes, shredded Mozzarella cheese, sliced Kalamata olives, and thinly sliced red onion over the pesto. If desired, add a handful of fresh arugula for a peppery touch.

Bake in the Oven:
- Place the pizza in the preheated oven and bake according to the pizza dough instructions or until the crust is golden, and the cheese is melted.

Finish and Serve:
- Once the pizza is done, remove it from the oven. If you like, sprinkle red pepper flakes over the top for a bit of heat. Slice and serve while warm.

Enjoy your Brazil Nut Pesto Pizza, a delightful combination of nutty pesto flavors with the freshness of pizza toppings!

Palm Heart and Bacon Pizza

Ingredients:

Pizza Dough:

- 1 pizza dough (store-bought or homemade)

Pizza Sauce:

- 1/2 cup tomato sauce
- 1 clove garlic, minced
- 1 teaspoon dried oregano
- Salt and black pepper to taste

Toppings:

- 1 cup Mozzarella cheese, shredded
- 1/2 cup cooked and crumbled bacon
- 1/2 cup palm hearts, sliced
- 1/4 cup red onion, thinly sliced
- 1/4 cup black olives, sliced
- Fresh basil leaves for garnish

Instructions:

Pizza Sauce:

Prepare Pizza Sauce:
- In a bowl, mix tomato sauce, minced garlic, dried oregano, salt, and black pepper. Set aside.

Pizza Assembly:

Preheat the Oven:
- Preheat your oven according to the pizza dough instructions, typically around 450°F (230°C).

Roll Out the Dough:
- Roll out the pizza dough on a floured surface to your preferred thickness.

Prepare the Pizza Pan:

- Place the rolled-out dough on a pizza pan or a baking sheet lined with parchment paper.

Spread Pizza Sauce:
- Evenly spread the prepared pizza sauce over the pizza dough, leaving a small border around the edges.

Add Cheese and Toppings:
- Sprinkle shredded Mozzarella cheese over the sauce. Distribute cooked and crumbled bacon, sliced palm hearts, thinly sliced red onion, and sliced black olives evenly over the cheese.

Bake in the Oven:
- Place the pizza in the preheated oven and bake according to the pizza dough instructions or until the crust is golden, and the cheese is melted.

Finish and Garnish:
- Once the pizza is done, remove it from the oven. Garnish with fresh basil leaves for a burst of flavor.

Slice and Serve:
- Slice the Palm Heart and Bacon Pizza into portions and serve while warm.

Enjoy your Palm Heart and Bacon Pizza, a delightful combination of savory bacon and the unique taste of palm hearts!

Coxinhas de Frango Pizza

Ingredients:

Pizza Dough:

- 1 pizza dough (store-bought or homemade)

Coxinhas de Frango Topping:

- 1 cup cooked and shredded chicken
- 1/2 cup cream cheese
- 1/4 cup mayonnaise
- 1/4 cup milk
- 1/4 cup green onions, finely chopped
- 1/4 cup cilantro, finely chopped
- 2 cloves garlic, minced
- Salt and pepper to taste

Toppings:

- 1 cup Mozzarella cheese, shredded
- 1/2 cup cheddar cheese, shredded
- 1/4 cup red bell pepper, diced
- 1/4 cup yellow bell pepper, diced
- 1/4 cup red onion, thinly sliced
- Sliced jalapeños (optional, for heat)

Instructions:

Coxinhas de Frango Topping:

Prepare Coxinhas de Frango Topping:
- In a bowl, combine shredded chicken, cream cheese, mayonnaise, milk, green onions, cilantro, minced garlic, salt, and pepper. Mix until well combined.

Pizza Assembly:

Preheat the Oven:

- Preheat your oven according to the pizza dough instructions, typically around 450°F (230°C).

Roll Out the Dough:
- Roll out the pizza dough on a floured surface to your preferred thickness.

Prepare the Pizza Pan:
- Place the rolled-out dough on a pizza pan or a baking sheet lined with parchment paper.

Spread Coxinhas de Frango Topping:
- Evenly spread the Coxinhas de Frango topping over the pizza dough, leaving a small border around the edges.

Add Cheese and Toppings:
- Sprinkle a combination of shredded Mozzarella and cheddar cheese over the chicken mixture. Add diced red and yellow bell peppers, thinly sliced red onion, and sliced jalapeños if you want some heat.

Bake in the Oven:
- Place the pizza in the preheated oven and bake according to the pizza dough instructions or until the crust is golden, and the cheese is melted and bubbly.

Finish and Serve:
- Once the Coxinhas de Frango Pizza is done, remove it from the oven. Slice and serve while warm.

Enjoy your Coxinhas de Frango Pizza, a fusion of the beloved Brazilian snack with the comfort of pizza!

Chocotone Dessert Pizza

Ingredients:

Pizza Dough:

- 1 pizza dough (store-bought or homemade)

Chocotone Spread:

- 1 cup chocotone crumbles (or chocolate panettone), finely chopped
- 1/4 cup chocolate hazelnut spread (e.g., Nutella)

Toppings:

- 1/2 cup white chocolate chips
- 1/4 cup dark chocolate chips
- 1/4 cup chopped nuts (e.g., hazelnuts or almonds)
- Powdered sugar for dusting
- Fresh berries for garnish (optional)

Instructions:

Chocotone Spread:

Prepare Chocotone Spread:
- In a bowl, combine finely chopped chocotone crumbles with chocolate hazelnut spread. Mix well to create a spreadable consistency.

Pizza Assembly:

Preheat the Oven:
- Preheat your oven according to the pizza dough instructions, typically around 450°F (230°C).

Roll Out the Dough:
- Roll out the pizza dough on a floured surface to your preferred thickness.

Prepare the Pizza Pan:
- Place the rolled-out dough on a pizza pan or a baking sheet lined with parchment paper.

Spread Chocotone Mixture:
- Evenly spread the chocotone mixture over the pizza dough, leaving a small border around the edges.

Add Chocolate and Nut Toppings:
- Sprinkle white chocolate chips, dark chocolate chips, and chopped nuts over the chocotone spread.

Bake in the Oven:
- Place the pizza in the preheated oven and bake according to the pizza dough instructions or until the crust is golden, and the chocolate is melted.

Finish and Garnish:
- Once the Chocotone Dessert Pizza is done, remove it from the oven. Dust with powdered sugar and garnish with fresh berries if desired.

Slice and Serve:
- Slice the Chocotone Dessert Pizza into portions and serve while warm.

Enjoy your Chocotone Dessert Pizza, a sweet and festive treat that combines the best of chocotone and pizza!

Brazilian Sausage and Banana Pizza

Ingredients:

Pizza Dough:

- 1 pizza dough (store-bought or homemade)

Pizza Sauce:

- 1/2 cup tomato sauce
- 1 clove garlic, minced
- 1 teaspoon dried oregano
- Salt and black pepper to taste

Toppings:

- 1 cup Mozzarella cheese, shredded
- 1/2 cup Brazilian-style sausage, cooked and crumbled
- 2 ripe bananas, sliced
- 1/4 cup red onion, thinly sliced
- 1/4 cup green bell pepper, thinly sliced
- 1/4 cup black olives, sliced
- Fresh cilantro for garnish

Instructions:

Pizza Sauce:

Prepare Pizza Sauce:
- In a bowl, mix tomato sauce, minced garlic, dried oregano, salt, and black pepper. Set aside.

Pizza Assembly:

Preheat the Oven:
- Preheat your oven according to the pizza dough instructions, typically around 450°F (230°C).

Roll Out the Dough:
- Roll out the pizza dough on a floured surface to your preferred thickness.

Prepare the Pizza Pan:

- Place the rolled-out dough on a pizza pan or a baking sheet lined with parchment paper.

Spread Pizza Sauce:
- Evenly spread the prepared pizza sauce over the pizza dough, leaving a small border around the edges.

Add Cheese and Toppings:
- Sprinkle shredded Mozzarella cheese over the sauce. Distribute cooked and crumbled Brazilian-style sausage, sliced bananas, thinly sliced red onion, green bell pepper, and sliced black olives evenly over the cheese.

Bake in the Oven:
- Place the pizza in the preheated oven and bake according to the pizza dough instructions or until the crust is golden, and the cheese is melted.

Finish and Garnish:
- Once the Brazilian Sausage and Banana Pizza is done, remove it from the oven. Garnish with fresh cilantro for a burst of flavor.

Slice and Serve:
- Slice the pizza into portions and serve while warm.

Enjoy your Brazilian Sausage and Banana Pizza, a delightful blend of savory and sweet flavors inspired by Brazilian cuisine!

Mandioca Pizza

Ingredients:

Cassava Crust:

- 2 cups cassava flour
- 1/4 cup olive oil
- 1 cup warm water
- 1 teaspoon salt

Pizza Sauce:

- 1/2 cup tomato sauce
- 1 clove garlic, minced
- 1 teaspoon dried oregano
- Salt and black pepper to taste

Toppings:

- 1 cup Mozzarella cheese, shredded
- 1/2 cup cooked and shredded chicken
- 1/4 cup red bell pepper, thinly sliced
- 1/4 cup green bell pepper, thinly sliced
- 1/4 cup black olives, sliced
- Fresh basil leaves for garnish

Instructions:

Cassava Crust:

Prepare Cassava Crust:
- In a large bowl, mix cassava flour, olive oil, warm water, and salt. Knead the mixture until you form a smooth dough.

Roll Out the Crust:
- Place the dough on a surface dusted with cassava flour. Roll out the dough to your preferred pizza crust thickness.

Prepare the Pizza Pan:
- Transfer the rolled-out cassava crust to a pizza pan or a baking sheet lined with parchment paper.

Pizza Sauce:

Prepare Pizza Sauce:
- In a bowl, mix tomato sauce, minced garlic, dried oregano, salt, and black pepper.

Pizza Assembly:

Preheat the Oven:
- Preheat your oven according to the pizza dough instructions, typically around 450°F (230°C).

Spread Pizza Sauce:
- Evenly spread the prepared pizza sauce over the cassava crust, leaving a small border around the edges.

Add Cheese and Toppings:
- Sprinkle shredded Mozzarella cheese over the sauce. Add cooked and shredded chicken, thinly sliced red and green bell peppers, and sliced black olives.

Bake in the Oven:
- Place the pizza in the preheated oven and bake according to the pizza dough instructions or until the crust is golden, and the cheese is melted.

Finish and Garnish:
- Once the Mandioca Pizza is done, remove it from the oven. Garnish with fresh basil leaves.

Slice and Serve:
- Slice the pizza into portions and serve while warm.

Enjoy your Mandioca Pizza, a gluten-free alternative with a Brazilian twist!

Brazilian-Style Vegetarian Pizza

Ingredients:

Pizza Dough:

- 1 pizza dough (store-bought or homemade)

Pizza Sauce:

- 1/2 cup tomato sauce
- 1 clove garlic, minced
- 1 teaspoon dried oregano
- Salt and black pepper to taste

Toppings:

- 1 cup Queijo Minas cheese (or substitute with mozzarella), shredded
- 1/2 cup hearts of palm, sliced
- 1/2 cup cherry tomatoes, halved
- 1/4 cup black olives, sliced
- 1/4 cup red onion, thinly sliced
- 1/4 cup green bell pepper, thinly sliced
- Fresh basil leaves for garnish

Instructions:

Pizza Sauce:

Prepare Pizza Sauce:
- In a bowl, mix tomato sauce, minced garlic, dried oregano, salt, and black pepper.

Pizza Assembly:

Preheat the Oven:
- Preheat your oven according to the pizza dough instructions, typically around 450°F (230°C).

Roll Out the Dough:
- Roll out the pizza dough on a floured surface to your preferred thickness.

Prepare the Pizza Pan:
- Place the rolled-out dough on a pizza pan or a baking sheet lined with parchment paper.

Spread Pizza Sauce:
- Evenly spread the prepared pizza sauce over the pizza dough, leaving a small border around the edges.

Add Cheese and Toppings:
- Sprinkle shredded Queijo Minas cheese (or mozzarella) over the sauce. Add sliced hearts of palm, halved cherry tomatoes, sliced black olives, thinly sliced red onion, and thinly sliced green bell pepper.

Bake in the Oven:
- Place the pizza in the preheated oven and bake according to the pizza dough instructions or until the crust is golden, and the cheese is melted.

Finish and Garnish:
- Once the Brazilian-Style Vegetarian Pizza is done, remove it from the oven. Garnish with fresh basil leaves.

Slice and Serve:
- Slice the pizza into portions and serve while warm.

Enjoy your Brazilian-Style Vegetarian Pizza, a burst of colors and flavors inspired by Brazilian cuisine!

Pork and Pineapple Pizza

Ingredients:

Pizza Dough:

- 1 pizza dough (store-bought or homemade)

Pizza Sauce:

- 1/2 cup tomato sauce
- 1 clove garlic, minced
- 1 teaspoon dried oregano
- Salt and black pepper to taste

Toppings:

- 1 cup Mozzarella cheese, shredded
- 1/2 cup cooked and shredded pork (such as ham or cooked pork loin)
- 1/2 cup pineapple chunks, fresh or canned
- 1/4 cup red onion, thinly sliced
- 1/4 cup bell peppers (a mix of red and green), thinly sliced
- Fresh cilantro or basil leaves for garnish

Instructions:

Pizza Sauce:

Prepare Pizza Sauce:
- In a bowl, mix tomato sauce, minced garlic, dried oregano, salt, and black pepper.

Pizza Assembly:

Preheat the Oven:
- Preheat your oven according to the pizza dough instructions, typically around 450°F (230°C).

Roll Out the Dough:
- Roll out the pizza dough on a floured surface to your preferred thickness.

Prepare the Pizza Pan:
- Place the rolled-out dough on a pizza pan or a baking sheet lined with parchment paper.

Spread Pizza Sauce:
- Evenly spread the prepared pizza sauce over the pizza dough, leaving a small border around the edges.

Add Cheese and Toppings:
- Sprinkle shredded Mozzarella cheese over the sauce. Add cooked and shredded pork, pineapple chunks, thinly sliced red onion, and thinly sliced bell peppers.

Bake in the Oven:
- Place the pizza in the preheated oven and bake according to the pizza dough instructions or until the crust is golden, and the cheese is melted.

Finish and Garnish:
- Once the Pork and Pineapple Pizza is done, remove it from the oven. Garnish with fresh cilantro or basil leaves.

Slice and Serve:
- Slice the pizza into portions and serve while warm.

Enjoy your Pork and Pineapple Pizza, a delightful balance of savory and sweet flavors!

Acarajé Inspired Pizza

Ingredients:

Pizza Dough:

- 1 pizza dough (store-bought or homemade)

Toppings:

- 1 cup black-eyed pea flour (fuba de feijão)
- 1/2 cup water
- 1 teaspoon salt
- Vegetable oil for frying
- 1/2 cup vatapá (a Brazilian sauce made from bread, shrimp, coconut milk, and spices)
- 1/2 cup peeled and cooked shrimp
- 1/4 cup diced tomatoes
- 1/4 cup thinly sliced green onions
- 1/4 cup chopped cilantro
- Sliced malagueta peppers or hot sauce (optional, for heat)

Instructions:

Black-eyed Pea Dough:

Prepare Black-eyed Pea Dough:
- In a bowl, mix black-eyed pea flour, water, and salt to form a thick, smooth dough.

Fry Acarajé Patties:
- Heat vegetable oil in a frying pan. Drop spoonfuls of the dough into the hot oil, frying until golden brown on both sides. Drain on paper towels.

Pizza Assembly:

Preheat the Oven:
- Preheat your oven according to the pizza dough instructions, typically around 450°F (230°C).

Roll Out the Dough:
- Roll out the pizza dough on a floured surface to your preferred thickness.

Prepare the Pizza Pan:
- Place the rolled-out dough on a pizza pan or a baking sheet lined with parchment paper.

Spread Vatapá on Dough:
- Spread a layer of vatapá over the pizza dough, leaving a small border around the edges.

Arrange Acarajé Patties:
- Place the fried acarajé patties evenly over the vatapá layer.

Add Shrimp and Toppings:
- Distribute peeled and cooked shrimp, diced tomatoes, thinly sliced green onions, and chopped cilantro over the pizza. If you enjoy some heat, add sliced malagueta peppers or drizzle with hot sauce.

Bake in the Oven:
- Place the pizza in the preheated oven and bake according to the pizza dough instructions or until the crust is golden, and the toppings are heated through.

Finish and Serve:
- Once the Acarajé Inspired Pizza is done, remove it from the oven. Slice and serve while warm.

Enjoy your Acarajé Inspired Pizza, a unique blend of flavors inspired by the beloved Brazilian street food acarajé!

Brigadeiro and Strawberry Dessert Pizza

Ingredients:

Pizza Dough:

- 1 pizza dough (store-bought or homemade)

Brigadeiro Sauce:

- 1 can (14 ounces) sweetened condensed milk
- 2 tablespoons unsweetened cocoa powder
- 2 tablespoons unsalted butter

Toppings:

- 1 cup fresh strawberries, hulled and sliced
- 1/2 cup white chocolate chips
- 1/4 cup shredded coconut, toasted
- Sweetened condensed milk (optional, for drizzling)

Instructions:

Brigadeiro Sauce:

Prepare Brigadeiro Sauce:
- In a saucepan, combine sweetened condensed milk, cocoa powder, and butter. Cook over medium heat, stirring continuously, until the mixture thickens and pulls away from the sides of the pan (similar to fudge consistency). Remove from heat and let it cool slightly.

Pizza Assembly:

Preheat the Oven:
- Preheat your oven according to the pizza dough instructions, typically around 450°F (230°C).

Roll Out the Dough:
- Roll out the pizza dough on a floured surface to your preferred thickness.

Prepare the Pizza Pan:
- Place the rolled-out dough on a pizza pan or a baking sheet lined with parchment paper.

Spread Brigadeiro Sauce:

- Spread the brigadeiro sauce evenly over the pizza dough, leaving a small border around the edges.

Add Strawberries and Toppings:
- Arrange sliced fresh strawberries over the brigadeiro sauce. Sprinkle white chocolate chips and toasted shredded coconut on top.

Bake in the Oven:
- Place the pizza in the preheated oven and bake according to the pizza dough instructions or until the crust is golden, and the toppings are slightly melted.

Finish and Drizzle:
- Once the Brigadeiro and Strawberry Dessert Pizza is done, remove it from the oven. If desired, drizzle with additional sweetened condensed milk for extra sweetness.

Slice and Serve:
- Slice the dessert pizza into portions and serve while warm.

Enjoy your Brigadeiro and Strawberry Dessert Pizza, a delightful treat that combines the rich flavor of brigadeiro with the freshness of strawberries!

Brazilian Caprese Pizza

Ingredients:

Pizza Dough:

- 1 pizza dough (store-bought or homemade)

Pesto Sauce:

- 1 cup fresh basil leaves
- 1/2 cup Brazil nuts, toasted
- 2 cloves garlic
- 1/2 cup Parmesan cheese, grated
- 1/2 cup extra-virgin olive oil
- Salt and black pepper to taste

Toppings:

- 1 cup Queijo Minas cheese (or substitute with mozzarella), shredded
- 1 cup cherry tomatoes, halved
- Balsamic glaze for drizzling
- Fresh basil leaves for garnish

Instructions:

Pesto Sauce:

Prepare Pesto Sauce:
- In a food processor, combine fresh basil leaves, toasted Brazil nuts, garlic, Parmesan cheese, salt, and black pepper. Pulse until coarsely ground.
- With the food processor running, gradually drizzle in the olive oil until the pesto reaches a smooth consistency. Adjust salt and pepper to taste. Set aside.

Pizza Assembly:

Preheat the Oven:
- Preheat your oven according to the pizza dough instructions, typically around 450°F (230°C).

Roll Out the Dough:
- Roll out the pizza dough on a floured surface to your preferred thickness.

Prepare the Pizza Pan:
- Place the rolled-out dough on a pizza pan or a baking sheet lined with parchment paper.

Spread Pesto Sauce:
- Evenly spread the prepared pesto sauce over the pizza dough, leaving a small border around the edges.

Add Cheese and Toppings:
- Sprinkle shredded Queijo Minas cheese (or mozzarella) over the pesto sauce. Distribute halved cherry tomatoes over the cheese.

Bake in the Oven:
- Place the pizza in the preheated oven and bake according to the pizza dough instructions or until the crust is golden, and the cheese is melted.

Finish and Garnish:
- Once the Brazilian Caprese Pizza is done, remove it from the oven. Drizzle with balsamic glaze and garnish with fresh basil leaves.

Slice and Serve:
- Slice the pizza into portions and serve while warm.

Enjoy your Brazilian Caprese Pizza, a delightful twist on the classic Caprese with the addition of Brazilian ingredients!

Guava and Cream Cheese Dessert Pizza

Ingredients:

Pizza Dough:

- 1 pizza dough (store-bought or homemade)

Cream Cheese Frosting:

- 8 ounces cream cheese, softened
- 1/2 cup powdered sugar
- 1 teaspoon vanilla extract

Toppings:

- 1 cup guava paste, sliced
- 1/2 cup fresh guava, sliced (optional)
- 1/4 cup shredded coconut, toasted
- Mint leaves for garnish (optional)

Instructions:

Cream Cheese Frosting:

Prepare Cream Cheese Frosting:
- In a bowl, beat together softened cream cheese, powdered sugar, and vanilla extract until smooth and creamy. Set aside.

Pizza Assembly:

Preheat the Oven:
- Preheat your oven according to the pizza dough instructions, typically around 450°F (230°C).

Roll Out the Dough:
- Roll out the pizza dough on a floured surface to your preferred thickness.

Prepare the Pizza Pan:
- Place the rolled-out dough on a pizza pan or a baking sheet lined with parchment paper.

Spread Cream Cheese Frosting:
- Evenly spread the cream cheese frosting over the pizza dough, leaving a small border around the edges.

Add Guava Toppings:
- Arrange sliced guava paste over the cream cheese frosting. If you have fresh guava, add slices as well.

Bake in the Oven:
- Place the pizza in the preheated oven and bake according to the pizza dough instructions or until the crust is golden and cooked through.

Finish and Garnish:
- Once the Guava and Cream Cheese Dessert Pizza is done, remove it from the oven. Sprinkle toasted shredded coconut over the top and garnish with mint leaves if desired.

Slice and Serve:
- Slice the dessert pizza into portions and serve while warm.

Enjoy your Guava and Cream Cheese Dessert Pizza, a tropical and sweet twist on the classic pizza concept!

Brazilian-Style Clam Pizza

Ingredients:

Pizza Dough:

- 1 pizza dough (store-bought or homemade)

Pizza Sauce:

- 1/2 cup tomato sauce
- 1 clove garlic, minced
- 1 teaspoon dried oregano
- Salt and black pepper to taste

Toppings:

- 1 cup Mozzarella cheese, shredded
- 1/2 cup cooked and chopped clams (canned or fresh)
- 1/4 cup red onion, thinly sliced
- 1/4 cup green bell pepper, thinly sliced
- 1/4 cup black olives, sliced
- 1/4 cup fresh cilantro, chopped
- Lemon wedges for serving

Instructions:

Pizza Sauce:

Prepare Pizza Sauce:
- In a bowl, mix tomato sauce, minced garlic, dried oregano, salt, and black pepper.

Pizza Assembly:

Preheat the Oven:
- Preheat your oven according to the pizza dough instructions, typically around 450°F (230°C).

Roll Out the Dough:
- Roll out the pizza dough on a floured surface to your preferred thickness.

Prepare the Pizza Pan:
- Place the rolled-out dough on a pizza pan or a baking sheet lined with parchment paper.

Spread Pizza Sauce:
- Evenly spread the prepared pizza sauce over the pizza dough, leaving a small border around the edges.

Add Cheese and Toppings:
- Sprinkle shredded Mozzarella cheese over the sauce. Distribute cooked and chopped clams, thinly sliced red onion, green bell pepper, sliced black olives, and fresh cilantro evenly over the cheese.

Bake in the Oven:
- Place the pizza in the preheated oven and bake according to the pizza dough instructions or until the crust is golden, and the cheese is melted.

Finish and Serve:
- Once the Brazilian-Style Clam Pizza is done, remove it from the oven. Serve with lemon wedges on the side for a burst of freshness.

Slice and Serve:
- Slice the pizza into portions and serve while warm.

Enjoy your Brazilian-Style Clam Pizza, a seafood delight with a touch of Brazilian flavor!

Chocolate and Coconut Dessert Pizza

Ingredients:

Pizza Dough:

- 1 pizza dough (store-bought or homemade)

Chocolate Sauce:

- 1/2 cup semisweet chocolate chips
- 1/4 cup heavy cream
- 2 tablespoons unsalted butter

Toppings:

- 1 cup sweetened shredded coconut, toasted
- 1/2 cup white chocolate chips
- 1/4 cup chopped almonds or hazelnuts, toasted
- Fresh strawberries or berries for garnish (optional)
- Powdered sugar for dusting

Instructions:

Chocolate Sauce:

Prepare Chocolate Sauce:
- In a small saucepan, heat the heavy cream until it just starts to simmer.
- Remove from heat and add chocolate chips and butter to the hot cream. Let it sit for a minute, then stir until smooth and well combined. Set aside to cool slightly.

Pizza Assembly:

Preheat the Oven:
- Preheat your oven according to the pizza dough instructions, typically around 450°F (230°C).

Roll Out the Dough:
- Roll out the pizza dough on a floured surface to your preferred thickness.

Prepare the Pizza Pan:

- Place the rolled-out dough on a pizza pan or a baking sheet lined with parchment paper.

Spread Chocolate Sauce:
- Evenly spread the prepared chocolate sauce over the pizza dough, leaving a small border around the edges.

Add Coconut and Toppings:
- Sprinkle toasted sweetened shredded coconut, white chocolate chips, and chopped toasted nuts over the chocolate sauce.

Bake in the Oven:
- Place the pizza in the preheated oven and bake according to the pizza dough instructions or until the crust is golden, and the chocolate is melted.

Finish and Garnish:
- Once the Chocolate and Coconut Dessert Pizza is done, remove it from the oven. If desired, garnish with fresh strawberries or berries and dust with powdered sugar.

Slice and Serve:
- Slice the dessert pizza into portions and serve while warm.

Enjoy your Chocolate and Coconut Dessert Pizza, a heavenly combination of chocolate and tropical coconut flavors!

Pão de Queijo Pizza Bites

Ingredients:

Pão de Queijo Dough:

- 2 cups tapioca flour
- 1 cup milk
- 1/2 cup unsalted butter
- 1 teaspoon salt
- 1 1/2 cups grated Parmesan cheese
- 1 cup shredded Mozzarella cheese
- 2 large eggs

Pizza Toppings:

- 1/2 cup tomato sauce
- 1 cup Mozzarella cheese, shredded
- 1/4 cup pepperoni slices (or other favorite pizza toppings)
- Fresh basil leaves for garnish

Instructions:

Pão de Queijo Dough:

Preheat the Oven:
- Preheat your oven to 375°F (190°C). Grease a mini muffin tin.

Prepare Pão de Queijo Dough:
- In a saucepan, combine milk, butter, and salt. Heat over medium heat until it comes to a simmer.
- In a large bowl, place tapioca flour. Pour the hot milk mixture over the tapioca flour and stir until well combined.
- Let the mixture cool slightly, then add grated Parmesan cheese, shredded Mozzarella cheese, and eggs. Mix until you have a smooth, thick dough.

Pizza Assembly:

Form Pão de Queijo Pizza Bites:
- Using a spoon or a cookie scoop, fill each mini muffin cup with the pão de queijo dough.

- Create a well in the center of each dough-filled cup, and add a small spoonful of tomato sauce, a sprinkle of shredded Mozzarella cheese, and a few pepperoni slices on top.

Bake in the Oven:
- Bake in the preheated oven for about 15-20 minutes or until the pão de queijo is puffed and golden.

Finish and Garnish:
- Once out of the oven, let the Pão de Queijo Pizza Bites cool slightly. Garnish with fresh basil leaves.

Serve:
- Remove the pizza bites from the muffin tin and arrange them on a serving platter. Serve warm.

Enjoy your Pão de Queijo Pizza Bites, a delicious blend of Brazilian and pizza flavors in a bite-sized form!

Brazilian Chicken Stroganoff Pizza

Ingredients:

Pizza Dough:

- 1 pizza dough (store-bought or homemade)

Chicken Stroganoff Sauce:

- 1 tablespoon olive oil
- 1 pound boneless, skinless chicken breast, thinly sliced
- 1 onion, finely chopped
- 2 cloves garlic, minced
- 1 tablespoon tomato paste
- 1 cup mushrooms, sliced
- 1/2 cup chicken broth
- 1 teaspoon paprika
- 1 teaspoon Dijon mustard
- 1 cup sour cream
- Salt and black pepper to taste

Toppings:

- 1 cup Mozzarella cheese, shredded
- 1/2 cup Parmesan cheese, grated
- Fresh parsley, chopped, for garnish

Instructions:

Chicken Stroganoff Sauce:

Prepare Chicken Stroganoff Sauce:
- In a large skillet, heat olive oil over medium heat. Add sliced chicken breast and cook until browned. Remove chicken from the skillet and set aside.
- In the same skillet, add chopped onion and garlic. Sauté until the onion is translucent.
- Stir in tomato paste, sliced mushrooms, chicken broth, paprika, and Dijon mustard. Cook until the mushrooms are tender.

- Add the cooked chicken back to the skillet and stir in sour cream. Season with salt and black pepper to taste. Simmer for a few minutes until the sauce thickens.

Pizza Assembly:

Preheat the Oven:
- Preheat your oven according to the pizza dough instructions, typically around 450°F (230°C).

Roll Out the Dough:
- Roll out the pizza dough on a floured surface to your preferred thickness.

Prepare the Pizza Pan:
- Place the rolled-out dough on a pizza pan or a baking sheet lined with parchment paper.

Spread Chicken Stroganoff Sauce:
- Evenly spread the prepared chicken stroganoff sauce over the pizza dough, leaving a small border around the edges.

Add Cheese and Toppings:
- Sprinkle shredded Mozzarella and grated Parmesan cheese over the chicken stroganoff sauce.

Bake in the Oven:
- Place the pizza in the preheated oven and bake according to the pizza dough instructions or until the crust is golden, and the cheese is melted.

Finish and Garnish:
- Once the Brazilian Chicken Stroganoff Pizza is done, remove it from the oven. Garnish with chopped fresh parsley.

Slice and Serve:
- Slice the pizza into portions and serve while warm.

Enjoy your Brazilian Chicken Stroganoff Pizza, a delicious blend of Brazilian and Italian flavors!

Chocotone Bread Pudding Pizza

Ingredients:

Pizza Dough:

- 1 pizza dough (store-bought or homemade)

Bread Pudding Filling:

- 4 cups chocotone, cubed (can also use panettone or any chocolate-filled sweet bread)
- 2 cups whole milk
- 4 large eggs
- 1/2 cup granulated sugar
- 1 teaspoon vanilla extract
- 1/2 teaspoon ground cinnamon
- 1/4 teaspoon nutmeg (optional)
- A pinch of salt

Streusel Topping:

- 1/2 cup all-purpose flour
- 1/4 cup granulated sugar
- 1/4 cup unsalted butter, cold and cubed

Optional Glaze:

- 1/2 cup powdered sugar
- 1-2 tablespoons milk
- 1/2 teaspoon vanilla extract

Instructions:

Bread Pudding Filling:

Prepare Bread Pudding Filling:
- In a bowl, whisk together eggs, sugar, vanilla extract, cinnamon, nutmeg (if using), and a pinch of salt.
- Gradually whisk in the milk until well combined.

- Add cubed chocotone to the egg mixture and gently toss to coat. Let it soak for about 15-20 minutes.

Streusel Topping:

Prepare Streusel Topping:
- In a bowl, combine flour, sugar, and cold cubed butter. Use your fingers or a pastry cutter to mix until it resembles coarse crumbs. Set aside.

Pizza Assembly:

Preheat the Oven:
- Preheat your oven according to the pizza dough instructions, typically around 450°F (230°C).

Roll Out the Dough:
- Roll out the pizza dough on a floured surface to your preferred thickness.

Prepare the Pizza Pan:
- Place the rolled-out dough on a pizza pan or a baking sheet lined with parchment paper.

Add Bread Pudding Filling:
- Spread the soaked chocotone mixture evenly over the pizza dough.

Sprinkle Streusel Topping:
- Sprinkle the streusel topping over the bread pudding mixture.

Bake in the Oven:
- Place the pizza in the preheated oven and bake according to the pizza dough instructions or until the crust is golden, and the bread pudding is set.

Optional Glaze:
- If desired, whisk together powdered sugar, milk, and vanilla extract to make a glaze. Drizzle the glaze over the warm pizza.

Slice and Serve:
- Slice the Chocotone Bread Pudding Pizza into portions and serve while warm.

Enjoy your Chocotone Bread Pudding Pizza, a festive and comforting dessert with Brazilian flair!

Tapioca Crust Pizza

Ingredients:

Tapioca Crust:

- 2 cups tapioca flour
- 1 cup water
- 1/4 cup olive oil
- 1 teaspoon salt

Pizza Sauce:

- 1/2 cup tomato sauce
- 1 clove garlic, minced
- 1 teaspoon dried oregano
- Salt and black pepper to taste

Toppings:

- 1 cup Mozzarella cheese, shredded
- Your favorite pizza toppings (e.g., pepperoni, mushrooms, bell peppers, olives, etc.)

Instructions:

Tapioca Crust:

Preheat the Oven:
- Preheat your oven to 450°F (230°C).

Prepare Tapioca Crust:
- In a saucepan, mix tapioca flour, water, olive oil, and salt over medium heat. Stir continuously until the mixture thickens and forms a dough-like consistency.
- Remove from heat and let it cool for a few minutes.
- Knead the dough until smooth. If it's too sticky, you can add a bit more tapioca flour.

Roll Out the Crust:
- Roll out the tapioca dough on a surface dusted with tapioca flour to prevent sticking. Roll it to your desired thickness.

Prepare the Pizza Pan:
- Place the rolled-out dough on a pizza pan or a baking sheet lined with parchment paper.

Pizza Sauce:

Prepare Pizza Sauce:
- In a bowl, mix tomato sauce, minced garlic, dried oregano, salt, and black pepper.

Pizza Assembly:

Spread Sauce on Tapioca Crust:
- Spread the pizza sauce evenly over the tapioca crust, leaving a small border around the edges.

Add Cheese and Toppings:
- Sprinkle shredded Mozzarella cheese over the sauce. Add your favorite pizza toppings.

Bake in the Oven:
- Place the pizza in the preheated oven and bake for approximately 12-15 minutes or until the crust is golden and the cheese is melted.

Finish and Serve:
- Once the Tapioca Crust Pizza is done, remove it from the oven. Let it cool for a few minutes before slicing.

Slice and Serve:
- Slice the pizza into portions and serve while warm.

Enjoy your Tapioca Crust Pizza, a gluten-free option with a chewy and satisfying texture!

Brazilian Chocolate and Banana Dessert Pizza

Ingredients:

Pizza Dough:

- 1 pizza dough (store-bought or homemade)

Chocolate Sauce:

- 1/2 cup semisweet chocolate chips
- 1/4 cup heavy cream
- 2 tablespoons unsalted butter

Toppings:

- 2 ripe bananas, sliced
- 1/4 cup chopped Brazil nuts (or walnuts)
- 1/4 cup sweetened condensed milk, for drizzling
- Powdered sugar, for dusting

Instructions:

Chocolate Sauce:

Prepare Chocolate Sauce:
- In a small saucepan, heat the heavy cream until it just starts to simmer.
- Remove from heat and add chocolate chips and butter to the hot cream. Let it sit for a minute, then stir until smooth and well combined. Set aside to cool slightly.

Pizza Assembly:

Preheat the Oven:
- Preheat your oven according to the pizza dough instructions, typically around 450°F (230°C).

Roll Out the Dough:
- Roll out the pizza dough on a floured surface to your preferred thickness.

Prepare the Pizza Pan:

- Place the rolled-out dough on a pizza pan or a baking sheet lined with parchment paper.

Spread Chocolate Sauce:
- Evenly spread the prepared chocolate sauce over the pizza dough, leaving a small border around the edges.

Add Banana and Nut Toppings:
- Arrange sliced bananas over the chocolate sauce. Sprinkle chopped Brazil nuts (or walnuts) on top.

Bake in the Oven:
- Place the pizza in the preheated oven and bake according to the pizza dough instructions or until the crust is golden, and the toppings are heated through.

Drizzle and Dust:
- Once the Chocolate and Banana Dessert Pizza is done, remove it from the oven. Drizzle sweetened condensed milk over the top and dust with powdered sugar.

Slice and Serve:
- Slice the dessert pizza into portions and serve while warm.

Enjoy your Brazilian Chocolate and Banana Dessert Pizza, a delightful combination of chocolatey goodness and tropical sweetness!

Caipirinha Pizza

Ingredients:

Pizza Dough:

- 1 pizza dough (store-bought or homemade)

Caipirinha Sauce:

- 1/2 cup cachaça (Brazilian sugarcane liquor)
- 1/4 cup fresh lime juice
- 1/4 cup simple syrup (equal parts sugar and water, dissolved together)
- Zest of one lime

Toppings:

- 1 cup Mozzarella cheese, shredded
- 1/4 cup fresh pineapple, diced
- 1/4 cup red onion, thinly sliced
- Fresh cilantro leaves for garnish

Instructions:

Caipirinha Sauce:

Prepare Caipirinha Sauce:
- In a small bowl, mix together cachaça, fresh lime juice, simple syrup, and lime zest. Set aside.

Pizza Assembly:

Preheat the Oven:
- Preheat your oven according to the pizza dough instructions, typically around 450°F (230°C).

Roll Out the Dough:
- Roll out the pizza dough on a floured surface to your preferred thickness.

Prepare the Pizza Pan:
- Place the rolled-out dough on a pizza pan or a baking sheet lined with parchment paper.

Spread Caipirinha Sauce:
- Evenly spread the prepared Caipirinha sauce over the pizza dough, leaving a small border around the edges.

Add Cheese and Toppings:
- Sprinkle shredded Mozzarella cheese over the sauce. Distribute diced fresh pineapple and thinly sliced red onion over the cheese.

Bake in the Oven:
- Place the pizza in the preheated oven and bake according to the pizza dough instructions or until the crust is golden, and the cheese is melted.

Garnish:
- Once the Caipirinha Pizza is done, remove it from the oven. Garnish with fresh cilantro leaves.

Slice and Serve:
- Slice the pizza into portions and serve while warm.

Enjoy your Caipirinha Pizza, a delicious blend of pizza and the vibrant flavors of the famous Brazilian cocktail!

Brazilian Nutella and Brigadeiro Dessert Pizza

Ingredients:

Pizza Dough:

- 1 pizza dough (store-bought or homemade)

Brigadeiro Sauce:

- 1 can (14 ounces) sweetened condensed milk
- 2 tablespoons unsweetened cocoa powder
- 2 tablespoons unsalted butter

Toppings:

- Nutella (as desired)
- Sliced bananas
- Chopped Brazil nuts or hazelnuts
- Shredded coconut (optional)
- Chocolate shavings (optional)

Instructions:

Brigadeiro Sauce:

Prepare Brigadeiro Sauce:
- In a saucepan, combine sweetened condensed milk, cocoa powder, and butter. Cook over medium heat, stirring continuously, until the mixture thickens and pulls away from the sides of the pan (similar to fudge consistency). Remove from heat and let it cool slightly.

Pizza Assembly:

Preheat the Oven:
- Preheat your oven according to the pizza dough instructions, typically around 450°F (230°C).

Roll Out the Dough:
- Roll out the pizza dough on a floured surface to your preferred thickness.

Prepare the Pizza Pan:

- Place the rolled-out dough on a pizza pan or a baking sheet lined with parchment paper.

Spread Brigadeiro Sauce:
- Spread the prepared brigadeiro sauce evenly over the pizza dough, leaving a small border around the edges.

Add Nutella and Toppings:
- Generously spread Nutella over the brigadeiro sauce. Arrange sliced bananas and chopped Brazil nuts (or hazelnuts) over the Nutella. Add shredded coconut and chocolate shavings if desired.

Bake in the Oven:
- Place the pizza in the preheated oven and bake according to the pizza dough instructions or until the crust is golden and the toppings are heated through.

Finish and Serve:
- Once the Brazilian Nutella and Brigadeiro Dessert Pizza is done, remove it from the oven. Let it cool for a few minutes.

Slice and Serve:
- Slice the dessert pizza into portions and serve while warm.

Enjoy your Brazilian Nutella and Brigadeiro Dessert Pizza, a heavenly combination of chocolatey delights!

Paçoca Dessert Pizza

Ingredients:

Pizza Dough:

- 1 pizza dough (store-bought or homemade)

Paçoca Cream:

- 1 cup sweetened condensed milk
- 1 cup creamy peanut butter
- 1/2 cup crushed paçoca (peanut candy)

Toppings:

- Sliced bananas
- Chopped roasted peanuts
- Chocolate drizzle (optional)
- Shredded coconut (optional)

Instructions:

Paçoca Cream:

Prepare Paçoca Cream:
- In a bowl, mix together sweetened condensed milk and creamy peanut butter until well combined.
- Crush paçoca into small pieces and fold it into the peanut butter mixture. Set aside.

Pizza Assembly:

Preheat the Oven:
- Preheat your oven according to the pizza dough instructions, typically around 450°F (230°C).

Roll Out the Dough:
- Roll out the pizza dough on a floured surface to your preferred thickness.

Prepare the Pizza Pan:

- Place the rolled-out dough on a pizza pan or a baking sheet lined with parchment paper.

Spread Paçoca Cream:
- Evenly spread the prepared paçoca cream over the pizza dough, leaving a small border around the edges.

Add Sliced Bananas and Peanuts:
- Arrange sliced bananas and chopped roasted peanuts over the paçoca cream.

Optional Toppings:
- If desired, drizzle chocolate over the pizza and sprinkle shredded coconut on top.

Bake in the Oven:
- Place the pizza in the preheated oven and bake according to the pizza dough instructions or until the crust is golden, and the toppings are heated through.

Finish and Serve:
- Once the Paçoca Dessert Pizza is done, remove it from the oven. Let it cool for a few minutes.

Slice and Serve:
- Slice the dessert pizza into portions and serve while warm.

Enjoy your Paçoca Dessert Pizza, a delightful fusion of the beloved Brazilian paçoca flavor in a creative pizza form!